# EVERYTHING DATA ANALYTICS: A BEGINNERS GUIDE TO DATA LITERACY

## UNDERSTANDING THE PROCESSES THAT TURN DATA INTO INSIGHTS

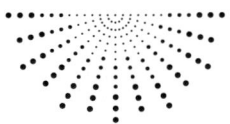

ELIZABETH CLARKE

# TABLE OF CONTENTS

# A Free Gift From Me to You!

# The Winning
# Data Visualization Checklist

Good     Average     Poor
☑       ☐       ☐

Make sure every visualization you create has all the elements that lead to a successful presentation!

Scan the QR code or visit ElizabethSClarke.com to get yours **Free!**

Download Here!

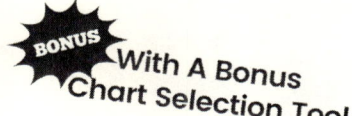

**BONUS** With A Bonus Chart Selection Tool

HOW TO PICK THE RIGHT CHART, THE FIRST TIME.

# INTRODUCTION

Data.

Just four letters, yet such a powerful word. Data is all around us. It is the foundation that every business sits on and without proper storage, development, analysis, and summarization of that data, that business's foundation will not hold strong. Data allows companies to make projections and develop goals for the future.

This is why over 74 zettabytes of data were produced in the year 2021 alone. 1 zettabyte is 1,000,000,000,000,000,000,000 bytes of data! That yearly figure is expected to grow to 175 zettabytes by 2025. This is because businesses revolve around data and its analysis and billions of dollars are being pumped into that industry. In fact, by the year 2023, it is expected that the data industry will be worth approximately $77 billion.

There are a few troubling statistics, though:

- About 80% of all data collected by companies are uninstructed and have not been interpreted for proper use.

- On average, most companies only analyze a little over 10% of the data that they receive. More than 80% of that data goes unused! So much insight remains unseen, which means, so much money is being left on the table.

Even though this industry is already worth billions of dollars, there is still so much room left for growth, improvement, and spending. That is where data professionals come together - to drive business decisions from structured data and make unstructured data pliable for companies to use in decision-making.

We have touched lightly upon why data is essential to every single organization in existence, but now the question is – why is it important to you, a blooming data professional? Hearing the word data can incite yawns in many people, but you are made of tougher stuff. You become excited, don't you? Because you see the value of this topic. Not only can you be one of the people filling the seats that need to be filled with the abundance of jobs in this industry, but you would also be paid handsomely to do so as there is so much demand. Data is everywhere, and someone needs to do the work of deciphering it and presenting it to other people in an easy-to-understand format. That is never going to change and therefore, there is so much potential for growth as a data professional. Not only can a career in this field be exciting, it can also offer a big incentive.

However, taking advantage of that opportunity can be challenging if you do not know where to start or how to gain the momentum you need. This book was written to give you that direction. Think of it as your compass to develop data literacy and guide you to gaining the skills that you need to be efficient and assured in your abilities.

However, we are getting ahead of ourselves and speaking about your future self, a confident and accomplished data professional. Currently, you might be feeling the pain of looking at career options and feeling intimidated. You may already be in a position, wanting to take that next step to excel in your career. You are not alone, and your feelings of trepidation are perfectly valid.

Yes, indeed, it can all seem overwhelming, take a moment and breathe. Take a deep inhalation and a slow exhalation. This book is going to take away that overwhelming sensation by taking all these unknowns and breaking them down into small, digestible pieces that allow you to take definitive steps in the right direction.

From the first chapter, you will gain valuable insights into what it means to be data literate and make a successful career out of data analytics. We will then touch on a familiar term known as "Data Science" and why it keeps getting thrown around. Before we get into the analysis process, we will cover fundamentals like "variables" and "data management systems." Once those systems are in place and the collection process begins, we can move into one of the most common tasks of the average data scientist, cleaning data. Only clean data has the capabilities to be appropriately analyzed, which will shortly follow the cleaning process. We will cover an exciting topic and an extremely useful tool known as "Business Intelligence (BI)," and much more, including machine learning algorithms for analysis, data visualization, big data, and job opportunities.

This book was written with the aim to give you everything you need to know about these aspects of data analytics and so much more. I am truly geeked out and fascinated by the way the world of data works. So, I have taken my fascination and many years of experience as a reputable marketer (where I analyze data and use data visualizations on a quarterly basis) to provide you with a compact guide for understanding and navigating this world of wonders.

I get it. I get *you*. I was overwhelmed when I first started wading through millions of bytes of data when I began my career. I didn't know where to start and I didn't know how to make them relate or connect. I certainly did not know how to find the causation for their existence. Learning what it all meant seemed an impossibility, mainly because it was so hard to find literature at the time that simplified the processes involved.

Through the confusion, I stuck with it because I was fascinated by how it all worked and how rewarding it would be to be one of the few people who understood what it all meant. The world of data amazes me, and I sense you feel the same way. Keep that passion for data. It will serve you well and guide you through that confusion. It has, after all, guided you to opening this book and reading so far.

That passion is why the book was written - my passion for helping other people who are also intrigued by data analytics. It was written to help people who are just starting out in this field and need easy-to-understand tools at their disposal to keep from being dissuaded from pursuing data analytics. It was written to be a simple yet effective guide for anyone to gain the data literacy they need and keep from being overwhelmed by all these bytes of data generated every day. It was created to let people who love data know what career options are available and what is required to pursue those careers.

No matter the global climate. No matter what the local economy says. No matter the current issues that plague a company, data analytics is always a vital part of engineering the way forward and you can be part of the few that pave the way. You can be someone who makes a positive impact from data.. Data analytics is always here to save the day, and you can be a hero in your own right. Best yet, there is an entire culture composed of people just like you here to support you. Turn the page to start your data analytics training!

# 1
# GETTING STARTED WITH DATA ANALYTICS

---

"Information is the oil of the 21st century, and analytics is the combustion engine."

— PETER SONDERGAARD

---

Data analytics is the broad term for turning data into insights. Formally defined, it is a network of processes and techniques focused on the analysis of raw sets of data so that concrete conclusions can be arrived at based on the information provided by that data. However, there is not one way to turn data into insights, there are many sub-disciplines that make this possible. There are three main components that make up data analytics:

## Data analysis

Data analysis is a process of inspecting, cleansing, transforming, and modeling data with the goal of discovering useful information, informing conclusions, and supporting decision-making.

**Data science**

Data science is an interdisciplinary field that uses scientific methods, processes, algorithms and systems, to extract knowledge and insights from noisy, structured, and unstructured data and apply knowledge and actionable insights from data across a broad range of application domains

**Big data**

Big data is a field that treats ways to analyze, systematically extract information from, or otherwise, deal with data sets that are too large or complex to be dealt with by traditional data-processing application software.

If data analytics is the pie, then data analysis, data science, and big data are the fruit inside. You need to be familiar with each of these components no matter what direction you go in this industry.

This chapter serves as an introduction to the field of data analytics and the tools, processes, and techniques that drive its functionality.

**What Exactly is Data Literacy?**

I'm sure you've seen this term thrown around, including in this book. Data literacy is the ability to collect, manage, analyze, and communicate data effectively to gain better business insights, leading to better business decisions.

**Processes of Data Analytics**

All businesses need to partake in the practice of data analytics. This examination of raw data allows companies to develop better strategies for pushing that business toward the ultimate goal of all companies: to grow, develop, and maximize profits. To that end, when data analytics is done correctly, it helps:

- Market more effectively

- Uncover business opportunities
- Make better decisions
- Find trends to follow
- Predict actions, triggers, or events that will affect the company

These benefits are only possible if those organizations follow the steps involved in the data analytics process. These steps include:

- Collect, organize, and manage the data

Companies are collecting data every single minute of the day. More than they can process, in fact, but you can never have enough when it comes to data. Knowing your customer can be the difference between significant gains or big losses. Companies collect data in many different ways, but internet tracking, social analytics, and transactional data are more common. This uncovers everything from customer purchases, interests, location, or behavior. The data collected needs to be organized to make the analysis process as easy as possible. Proper data management and storage are essential, especially in larger companies, when amassing incredible amounts of data every day. Systems need to be in place to keep everything running smoothly.

- Clean the data

Uncleaned data is data whereby certain details overlap or are missing. Such data is not helpful as it does not provide a complete picture that allows for sound decision-making to occur. Anything that overlaps needs to be rectified, and incomplete information must be supplemented with whatever is missing. There is also the aspect of eliminating any mistakes that might have happened during the data collection and organization processes. Data can be considered clean and useful only after these processes have been done.

- Analyze the data

Understanding and engaging the bytes of information sets the foundation for dissecting this data. This process of dissection is analyzing the data. Analyzation allows for the shift of focus from collecting the data to discovering insights available from the data. Many techniques and processes can be learned to find information from large sets of data. Some include machine learning techniques like classification or clustering. The goal is to find patterns, trends, outliers, or anything else that will give you valuable information. We will cover some common techniques in chapter 8.

- Interpret and visualize the data

Data is simply that, data. Bytes of information, numbers, statistics. What does it mean? Without understanding it, there isn't much use for it. After the analysis, you will be left with insights and outliers that only some will understand at a glance. (Most likely still in a spreadsheet of data) Data visualization is how you can turn a set of numbers into an understandable presentation from which employees can take action. With this understanding, better business decisions can be made.

WHEN THESE STEPS are followed correctly, companies can make educated decisions based on facts and not guesses. For example, companies can monitor customer behavior and preferences and ensure they continue to provide them with similar products or services to keep them happy and engaged. Similar to what Netflix does with your show suggestions or Amazon with your product suggestions.

This book will take you through the processes of data analytics and help you enhance your data literacy to strive in such an important industry.

## 2
# WHAT EXACTLY IS DATA SCIENCE?

"Data science is all about asking interesting questions based on the data you have, or often the data you don't have."

— SARAH JAVIS

M any terms are being thrown around in the world of data, and data science is one of them. I'm sure some of you are wondering what this means and why you keep seeing it. Well, Data science is a field of study that uses algorithms, systems, statistics and more to extract insights from data. For reference, a data analyst usually works with structured data to solve business problems and gain insights using Python, and SQL. Well, a data scientist tends to be off in the unknown, using more advanced techniques to make predictions for the future from raw data. They could potentially set up unsupervised machine learning algorithms or predictive modeling processes (these terms will become more familiar as you read on). I like to consider a data scientist an upgraded version of a data analyst. They still analyze and work with data, just in a more advanced way. Data scientists usually work for larger companies and work with larger sets of unstructured Big Data. Let's briefly go through the main components of data science so you have a better understanding of this common term.

## 5 MAIN COMPONENTS OF DATA SCIENCE

There are a few basic concepts we need to understand that make up this field of study. It will also help you wrap your head around some common terms to better understand the concepts of this book. These components are as follows:

1. **Structured and Unstructured Data**

Structured data refers to organized and formatted data that is easily searchable through machine language. Examples of data items in this category include addresses, names, and dates.

There is a subset of structured data called semi-structured data. This type of data does not conform to the typical tabular structure of structured data. Still, it contains features that make it fit within a database—email databases, web pages and HTML fall under this type of data structure.

Unstructured data refers to information that is not arranged to a specific data model and cannot be stored in a traditional database. The processing of unstructured data needs a bit of human intuition and opinion. Examples of unstructured data include video clips, social media activity, audio clips and text messages.

For now, we are only skimming the surface of structured and unstructured data to understand the terminology. We will look at some examples and get a better understanding in chapter 3, data storage.

## 1. Machine Learning

As mentioned previously, machine learning is essentially algorithms that allow the processing of sets of data without human handling. These systems are driven by algorithms or rules that allow large volumes of data to be processed and refined in a uniform and structured way.

Machine learning is used to analyze patterns, make predictions, and give recommendations. We will focus more deeply on machine learning later.

## 1. Statistics and Probability

Statistics refers to the mathematical application of collecting, analyzing, interpreting, and presenting data in a numerical form. Probability speaks to the extent to which something is likely to occur. Probabilities are measured with ratios to show that extent. These applications provide insight and likelihood and thus, provide the numerical foundation that drives decision-making and strategic planning in data science. Although not necessary to master right away, there is a bonus chapter on statistics at the end of the book if you would like to understand it a bit more.

## 1. Programming Languages

Data is largely processed by computers in this day and age, and these computers speak their own unique languages. These languages include:

*SQL*

SQL stands for structured query language. It is a programming language used most often to manage tabular or relational databases.

This programming language is the opposite of NoSQL, which is a language that allows for the storage and processing of data that falls outside of that tabular structure.

Examples of SQL databases are Oracle, Access and Microsoft SQL server. Learning SQL is an essential skill for a data scientist.

*Python*

This is the most popular programming language among data scientists. Even though this is a high-level language, its popularity is attributed to its high readability and the ease with which it can be used in both large-scale and smaller projects. In other words, it is a great tool for beginners to use. One of the features that make this a beginner-friendly tool is that it is object-oriented. This means that everything created in Python is perpetrated as an object. All of these objects have different properties, making them easy to identify and operate.

Another feature that makes this easy to use is that its system uses English words and basic symbols. Users do not have to be an expert at coding languages to learn this.

It is also cost-effective as it can be integrated with other software and third-party components like API (Application Programming Interface) as well other programming languages like C++, Rust and Java. Python is also easy to integrate with existing databases like customer lists as most people and businesses are not starting from scratch when they start using this programming language. As a result of this seamless integration across so many platforms, Python can be the glue that holds it together. It is a far better alternative to attempting to piece everything together or dumping it all to use one brand's products.

Python is often used to develop websites, software, and apps in addition to conducting data analysis. If a data scientist or business is indeed starting from scratch, Python can be used to create databases. Other uses include:

- Conducting simulations
- Automating reports
- Creating predictive models
- Doing academic research

If you are a beginner to Python but want to get your feet wet quickly, here are a few things that I would advise you to learn:

## Data Types

These are the classification of data items. Data types in Python include:

- Integers, which are a number classification with no maximum limit to the value of the number. These are whole numbers.
- Strings, which are lines of characters represented by single, double, or triple quotes. (NORWAY, XX777, 12/12/2024)
- Floating point numbers, which is a number classification that uses decimal points to show no maximum limit to the value of the number.

### Loops and Conditionals

Despite the extreme readability of python, it's recommended that you understand what loops are (the execution of blocks of code several times) and what conditions are (the commands that tell loops when to stop repeating).

### Learn How to Manipulate Data

The best way to do this is to learn how to read the data stored in the Python program. Despite the fact that this tool makes it easy for you, you will want to get down and dirty with cleaning up data, doing calculations, and doing all the other work that goes into manipulating data. Do not let the use of technology turn you into a lazy data scientist!

Although I can't make you a Python and SQL expert in this book as we have a broad array of topics to cover, it's worth investing in a program or course with hands-on projects. This is the best way to learn Python and SQL, in my opinion. There are many jobs in data, some with interchangeable skills and some with fewer entry barriers. It's necessary to assess your career goals, what skill sets are required for said goals, and then decide what is worth investing in and what isn't.

## Guidelines to follow when learning python programming

**Step 1:** The basics

You should start by learning the basics of the language, libraries, and data structures. A great way to do this is to take an online course through Udemy or Coursera. They offer great beginner to advanced programs on many data related topics.

**Step 2:** Learn regular expressions in Python

You will need to use them for data cleansing, especially if you are working on text data. There are also great online courses specifically specializing in regular expressions.

**Step 3:** Learn Scientific libraries in Python – NumPy, SciPy, Matplotlib, and Pandas

Here is a brief introduction to the various libraries:

- Practice NumPy thoroughly, especially NumPy arrays. This will form a good foundation for things to come.

- Next, look up SciPy Tutorials. There is a lot of free content available. Find an introductory course to learn the basics and go from there.
- Finally, let us look at Pandas. Pandas provides DataFrame functionality (like R) for Python. This is also where you should spend a good time practicing. Pandas would become the most effective tool for all mid-size data analysis. Start with a short introduction, then move on to more advanced/hands-on training. Either through free content online or the many courses available. There's no shortage of data science-related content online nowadays.

**Step 4:** Data visualization

Learn how to create effective data visualizations, to turn your insights into valuable information. There will be more information on various programs to use in chapter 10.

**Step 5:** Learn Scikit-learn and machine learning

Although this is more advanced, Scikit-learn is the most useful library on python for machine learning. It's also great to go through lectures/courses with assignments attached. Supervised learning algorithms like regressions and non-supervised learning algorithms like clustering. (Which we will briefly cover later).

**Step 6:** Practice!

Work on a variety of different projects to expand your knowledge.

If you need a guideline on where to get started for more advanced training, Join my email list at ElizabethSClarke.com and reply to the first message with your needs. I will happily guide you in the right direction with some great free content and course suggestions.

Although this is a brief introduction, I hope it points your compass in the right direction and gets you started on your python journey.

## 5. Big Data

We have come to the 5$^{th}$ main component of data science, which is big data. The definition of big data is revealed in the name. It is data that contains a wide variety of information, coming at an increase in velocity. Big data is larger and more complex than your run-of-the-mill data. Examples include social media websites and stock exchanges. Large companies like Netflix or Meta are good examples, as they collect unfathomable amounts of data every day.

Big data consists of unstructured, structured, and semi-structured data and it is used for driving machine learning projects, data modelling, and advanced analytics applications.

We will focus more deeply on big data later in the book.

# 3
# UNDERSTANDING VARIABLES

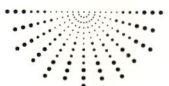

"Errors using inadequate data are much less than those using no data at all."

— CHARLES BABBAGE

I n the world of data analytics, there are some fundamentals everyone must know. Variables are one of them. We know that data can be structured, unstructured, and semistructured, but if we dive deeper into the details of that data, you'll find they are made up of numerical and categorical values, which we call variables. Variables identify the data to be understood by algorithms and accessed for future analysis.

Variables can be length, time, price, diameter, date, strength, temperature, and more. Let's look at this customer order spreadsheet for reference.

| Customer No. | Order No. | Order Date | Product Sku | QTY | Product Cost | Total |
|---|---|---|---|---|---|---|
| 00865 | 708900 | 6-Feb-22 | ZG011AQA | 2 | $49.99 | $99.98 |
| 00779 | 708901 | 6-Feb-22 | GH77HRU | 7 | $29.95 | $209.65 |
| 00669 | 708902 | 6-Feb-22 | ZG011AQA | 3 | $49.99 | $149.97 |
| 00079 | 708903 | 7-Feb-22 | JJ955RUR | 1 | $139.99 | $139.99 |
| 00447 | 708904 | 7-Feb-22 | JK88JJM | 19 | $14.50 | $275.50 |
| 00125 | 708905 | 8-Feb-22 | GH77HRU | 6 | $29.95 | $179.70 |
| 00777 | 708906 | 8-Feb-22 | LL65LLK | 17 | $19.95 | $339.15 |

**FIGURE 3.1** Everything in this table is considered a variable

## Independent and Dependent Variables

As we dove into the details of data to discover it is made up of variables, you'll learn they are either independent or dependent if you dive even deeper. Independent variables (Known as X) are responsible for determining the value of the dependent variables (Known as y). If you're analyzing a student's average test score (dependant variable), the result is determined by how much the person studies (independent variable). Understanding the relationships between the variables allows you to make desired changes and predict certain outcomes. As we go further into data science, you'll learn that this is the basic model for machine learning and algorithms. The independent variable is considered the "Input," and the dependant variable the "Output." Machines learn the relationship between these two and run "models" to predict future outputs.

## Types of Variables

There are four main types of variables in data analytics that one must be familiar with.

1. Categorical
2. Numerical
3. Date/Time
4. Boolean

## Categorical Variables

Categorical Variables can be divided into two main subcategories:

1. Ordinal
2. Nominal

As they sound, ordinal variables have a natural categorical order to them. Examples of ordinal variables would be income level (40-70k, over 100k) rating (satisfactory, good, great), days of the week, or anything alike. Nominal variables, however, are the opposite, with no order associated with them. This could be gender, city names, operating systems, zip codes, eye color, etc. Although categorical variables are strings of letters, they can sometimes be expressed as a number for the purpose of statistics. Still, these numbers won't have the same meaning as a numerical value. E.g., medicine 1, medicine 2, zipcodes, etc.

## Numerical Variables

As categorical variables are divided into two subcategories, numerical variables do the same. They are divided into:

1. Discrete
2. Continuous

Discrete numerical variables contain only a discrete quantity known as integers. This would be a whole number (1, 11, 111). Examples include the number of houses someone owns, the number of purchases from a customer, or the number of products a company sells. Continuous variables, however, fill in the void. Showcasing continuous quantities or fractional quantities. E.g., Customer transactions ($725.67) or average time customers spend on a website (14.76 seconds).

*QUICK TIP: "CATEGORICAL" and "date/time" variables are generally categorized as "Discrete" values.*

. . .

## Date/Time

Date/time variables are relatively simple. They mark the date or time. Examples would be transaction history (Date of order), clock in time of an employee, birthdates, etc.

## Boolean Variables

A boolean variable is a variable that can be 1 of 2 outcomes (0/1, true/false, yes/no)

They can often be overlapped with categorical variables. For example, if you're determining who owns which vehicle, you could categorize Audi as (0) and Lexus as (1), as long as you compare only two values. This can also make it easier for algorithms to analyze large data sets.

Having a general understanding of variables will give you a strong foundation that will be necessary for many data-related tasks you may come across.

# 4

# DATA COLLECTION

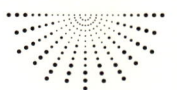

---

"With data collection 'The sooner the better' is always the best answer."

— MARISSA MAYER

---

**H**oarding.

This sounds like an unpleasant word to my ear. That might be because it incites an image of junk threatening to bury anyone who dares to walk by it. The word incites the same image in my head regarding data collection - one where the data analyst mentally gets buried by tons of information. Not every single byte of information is useful for reaching conclusive insights. That is the data collection process needs to be approached in a way that makes the data professionals' job more accessible rather than one where they will need help to become unburied.

## The Goal of Data Collection

There needs to be an end goal for the collection process. This can be decided at the analyst level before infiltrating some databases or at a big business level when they set up data management systems to encapsulate customer information. To determine that end goal, you need to ask yourself a few questions. Answering these questions will help define what your goal for data collection is. Such questions include:

- What is the current situation and where is it happening?
- Why is this situation occurring?
- What is the data going to be used for?
- Why is it being collected?
- How will it be useful?
- Whom will it be useful to?

Answering these questions will allow the development of a plan of attack for approaching the data collection to support these questions. It allows for awareness of the problem or opportunity. It defines that problem or opportunity instead of having a vague or obscure notion of why you engage in this process. To be clear, a problem and an opportunity have something in common, and that is they represent the difference between the current situation and desired outcome. You would like to move from point A to point B. Data collection is the vessel that moves you between these points. But first, there needs to be a brainstorming session that presents possible routes for moving between these two points. Only after this brainstorming session occurs can you then move on to how this vessel will be designed. The design of this vessel is the particular method of data collection that will be used. This is why Netflix collects data such as time spent watching a show, so they know to recommend more of what you are actually watching, not recommendations based on shows you tried out but didn't like. Collecting the right data is important.

## Different Types of Data Collection

Data collection is not a one size fits all kind of deal. What might be appropriate in one instance might lead to a headache in another instance. For example, falling back on your vessel analogy, let's say you want to take a leisurely boat ride across a pond, a cargo ship will not be suitable. It might even destroy the setting because of its size and power. However, a rowboat will certainly be more effective in creating the end goal which is a relaxing ride.

The same applies to data collection. The method of collection needs to align with the goal of its collection. The first step in choosing the right method of data collection is to know what the options are. Let's discuss these options now.

There are two main forms of data collection. They are:

- Primary data collection
- Secondary data collection

## Primary Data Collection

Let's look at primary data collection first. This type of data collection is the one where the data is collected directly from the source about which that data is being developed. There are two types of primary data collection methods. They are:

- Qualitative research method
- Quantitative research method

The qualitative research method measures the intangible components of the data gathered. Such tangible items include feelings and sentiments. There are no figures included in this data collection method, so this method is developed around descriptions instead of numeric values.

An example of qualitative data collection is a customer's review after buying a product. This customer might say they loved, hated, or simply had a satisfactory experience using the product. As a result, the data collected is not easily measured; there is no real measure of a person's feelings toward the product.

So how is qualitative data useful?

The answer to this is that this kind of data is great for finding the causation of the data received. The customer is likely not to express only their feelings about the product but also why they feel that way.

Where qualitative data falls short, quantitative data picks up the slack. Quantitative data are measurable items given in figures, numbers, and quantities. The quantitative aspect would be the customer's product rating (e.g., 4 stars). Other quantitative data items will be how long this customer spent on the website if this shopping experience happened on an e-commerce store, how many other customers have also bought this product and how the product scores compared to similar products.

Qualitative data is excellent so you can uncover information about the customer. In contrast, the measurable qualities provided by quantitative data allow for gaining an objective insight into which reliable decision-making can be done. Quantitative and qualitative data go hand in hand. Quantitative data sets the foundation with figures and other measurable items, which is supplemented with the why these measures exist with qualitative data. As should be noted, both of these types of data are collected directly from the source. The customer is a direct source of information about their feelings about the product purchased. The website analytics of the e-commerce store is a direct source of information about visitor behavior.

**Secondary Data**

Secondary data is qualitative or quantitative data previously gathered by another person, institution, or organization, in the past, usually for a different purpose, such as reporting or research, which will most likely be kept in a database that you can access. If you need to gather secondary data, there are some things you need to consider.

1. Evaluating and stating the purpose of getting this supportive data. There needs to be a clearly stated understanding of why the collection of this data is being pursued. This prevents data hoarding and gives clear direction in the collection process.

2. The development of a data design plan. This plan needs to include:

- Where the data will be sourced.
- The type of data that will be sourced, quantitative or qualitative.
- The method by which the data will be collected.
- The tools that will be used for the collection.
- How the collected data will be analyzed.

3. The development of research questions will validate the secondary data collected. This step is necessary for authenticating the data collected as relevant, reputable, and unbiased.

4. Locating the secondary data. With the design plan and research questions in hand, you can then identify the secondary data. This location is vital as only reputable sources need to be used. Also, it needs to be clear whether or not the data source is quantitative, qualitative, or both.

5. Evaluation of the secondary data collected. The stage serves to validate the data gathered to note whether or not it has fulfilled its intended purpose.

### Data Collection Methodologies

Whether the data type is primary or secondary, there are a few standard methods by which data is collected. It is important first to understand the systems in place that are built to manage large quantities of data that companies collect everyday. A data architect's primary role is to create blueprints for data management systems. After they assess a company's data sources (internal and external), architects put together a plan that effectively integrates, centralizes, protects and ultimately maintains the system. Their goal is to allow employees to access crucial company information with ease. Effective data management follows a particular pathway. Different businesses and organizations have their own particular needs and need to cater that pathway to reach their goals, but a general pathway looks like this:

## The data architecture

The data architecture describes the collection, organization, integration and storage plan. It is introduced at the beginning of the data analysis process as it sets the stage for everything else that will follow. Just like you will not build the foundation or the roof of a building without the architectural plan in place, the same applies to data. The architecture sets a precedent for everything else.

## The data model

This describes how the structure of a database will be modeled. Data models define how the data relate to one other, how it processes and where it gets stored within the system.

## The data integration system

Data integration is how data from all different business systems and formats get combined into a single unified view. This then gets stored in a data warehouse.

## The quality check system

The quality check identifies and removes inconsistencies and errors in the data that have been collected. This part of the system will also ensure that no information is missing, and if this is found, that information will be promptly sourced. This pathway of the data management process activates cleanup tasks.

## The data governance system

The governance system is the pathway that sets the rules that will guide the entire analysis process management. It ensures that consistency remains from start to finish and that the parameters of the data gathering, collection, integration and storage processes are obeyed. It also determines who has authority and control of the data and its use. As a data scientist or data analyst, you will simply be gaining access to this data to make sense of it.

The process usually starts with the data architect designing the blueprint for the system. It then moves to the data engineer, which brings the blueprints to life. For the data scientists and analysts to access this data, the data engineers move and transform it into data "pipelines" that get the data to the scientists and analysts. Data pipelines transfer data between a source system and a target repository.

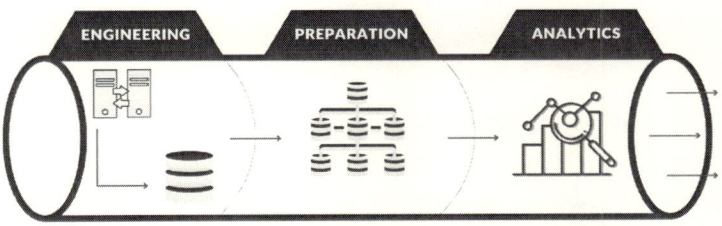

**FIGURE 4.1**

Now that we understand the systems that allow companies to keep track of their data, how are they collecting it? Some data collection methods include:

## Online Forms and Questionnaires

Widely used because it is so effective at collecting both quantitative and qualitative data, forms and questionnaires facilitate the collection of data by asking questions in an effort to gain key insights through unbiased answers. Examples of tools used in this methodology of data collection are Google Forms and Type-form. It is more typical to see closed-ended questions used in forms and questionnaires as this places parameters around the data collected. For example, if a form asks *How satisfied are you with the product?* The possible answers for this include may include:

1. Very satisfied
2. Satisfied
3. Somewhat satisfied
4. Dissatisfied

This prevents the collection of data that is irrelevant to the intended purpose of gathering that set of data. This also limits the cleanup process necessary for making this data usable.

## Internet Tracking

If we think about it too deeply, the amount of information gathered about everyone who uses devices connected to the internet is alarming. Someone's social media activities, the websites they frequent most often and the type of content they enjoy watching and reading are just a few of the data points accumulated as we enjoy using them.

This data is useful to us in many contexts as it allows more relevant content to come up on our social media feeds and as the recommended items on many of our most loved internet activities.

It is also an excellent avenue for companies to understand individual and consumer needs. These companies can gather this data using tools known as cookies and tracking pixels. It should be noted that you do have the option to disable at least some of the functionalities of such tools in your internet browsers.

## Web-Based Marketing Analytics

Marketing without tracking the reactions of the intended consumer is highly ineffective as it does not allow for fine-tuning the processes to better reach and entice the target market. In the day and age that we live in, billboards and posters are not the only avenues for reaching target markets and often they are not the most efficient for getting the audience to act as desired. Web-based marketing techniques like the use of social media are far more efficient. Selling a product to a consumer or getting a person to sign up for a newsletter is just one click away.

As a result of this, there is a plethora of data that can be gathered based on consumer behavior and how they respond to particular web-based marketing techniques. Such data includes how frequently a specific ad gets clicked on, the times of day it's viewed, regions where it gets most visibility and how long the viewer engages with the ad.

The great thing is that social media platforms and personal web development allow you to easily access this information with an analytics feature. As easy as can be, the data, which is more often quantitative, is right there at the data professional's fingertips.

## Social Media Monitoring

Social media is a major part of the marketing focus of any company in this digital day and age. Qualitative data is available in statistical, percentages and numeric forms. They provide data on how often content is engaged with. From these metrics tailored marketing, consumer retention, and audience outreach strategies can be developed to ensure higher conversions.

Qualitative data can also be derived from comments and remarks.

## Transactional Data

Transactional data can benefit a company as it tells them exactly what people buy. This information can be used for email campaigns so 1:1 outreach is more effective with targeted discounts. It can also determine a campaign's success, your best and worst customers and everything in between. This makes targeting lookalike customers easier, which is essential to creating loyal customers, not one-time buyers.

Collecting consumer data helps a wide range of companies better understand their customers to provide better services for those customers. Now that we've collected the data, I think it's time we understand how to store it.

5

# DATA STORAGE

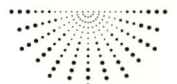

---

"Data that is loved tends to survive."

— KURT BOLLACKER

---

Data is comparable to having gold in the business world. This is why so much of it is collected; because every byte of it has the potential to fatten up many bank accounts and continue to do so for decades and centuries after it was collected. Therefore, just like you would not leave a nugget of gold just sitting out in the open for anyone to potentially pick up, businesses also should not leave data where anyone can grab it and disappear with it.

Storage is one of the first steps that needs urgent consideration when it comes to data security. Before we get that, though, let's get into a formal definition of data storage. Data storage is the physical means used to hold data to remain accessible when needed.

Efficient data storage gives a healthy balance between security and accessibility. It does no good to data analysts and other business professionals who use this data if they feel like they have to jump through hoops just to access it. Before we find out about storage methods, we must first understand the three main categories of data and their characteristics. These 3 are Unstructured, Semi-Structured, and Structured data.

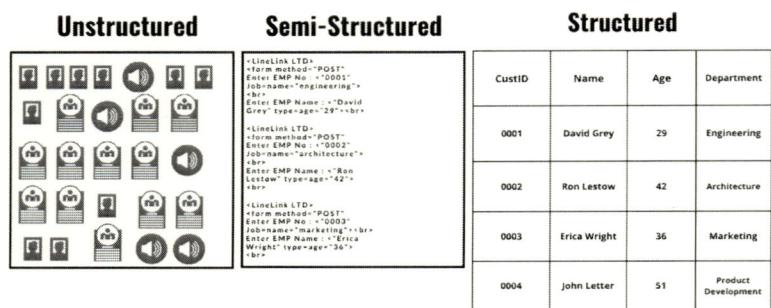

**FIGURE 5.0**

## Unstructured Data

Unstructured data is exactly how it sounds, data that is in multiple formats and has no specific organization or structure to it. Unstructured data is essentially any data that doesn't fit nicely into a spreadsheet. Anywhere from videos clips to pdfs, images and audio files. Unstructured data is challenging for a computer to make sense of. This is why data scientists will often use more advanced techniques and even AI (Artificial intelligence) to organize and make sense of this data. Unstructured data can be stored in applications such as NoSQL. This database is non-tabular and therefore perfect for holding this type of data. A non-tabular or non-relational database is a database that does not use standard columns and rows. It uses a storage model with specific requirements based on the data being stored. Another example of this would be a data lake.

Unstructured data makes up 80% of all data. Although difficult to work with, unstructured data is widespread and essential to businesses. New processes and techniques are being implemented consistently to work with this type of data efficiently.

## Semi-Structured Data

Semi-structured data falls right in the middle. It's not as organized as structured data but isn't as chaotic as unstructured data. It doesn't entirely obey the tabular structure of databases the same way structured data does. Still, it does contain tags or other markers to separate essential elements and categorize the information roughly. An example could be data in an HTML format. The information is there, but it is not in as organized of a format as it should be and is not quite readable by algorithms. It needs some slight processing.

## Structured Data

Structured data refers to organized and formatted data easily searchable through machine language (algorithms , etc). A well-organized excel spreadsheet is a great example. The reason structured data is so valuable to data professionals is they can easily use it for data visualizations, data analytics and machine learning models without any extensive pre-processing. It is often in tabular form, storing it in tables and rows where you can update multiple rows simultaneously. This can be useful for removing commas or anything that isn't easily read by machine learning algorithms. It also proves helpful when you want to designate a specific feature, such as people living in a particular area or country. You can filter out anyone who doesn't meet your desired requirements. Although structured data is desired, it only makes up about 20% of all data.

## TYPES OF DATA STORAGE

### Relational Database

A relational database organizes structured data into tables linked based on pre-defined relationships. The tables will be linked using keys. A primary key will identify each row. This key can be added to another table, making it a foreign key. The relationships between the primary key and foreign key form the basis of how the database works. This allows you to retrieve data from multiple tables with a single query (a query is a request for data or information from a database table or combination of tables.) It can be advantageous when companies want to understand better relationships among data and gain valuable insights that lead to better decision-making.

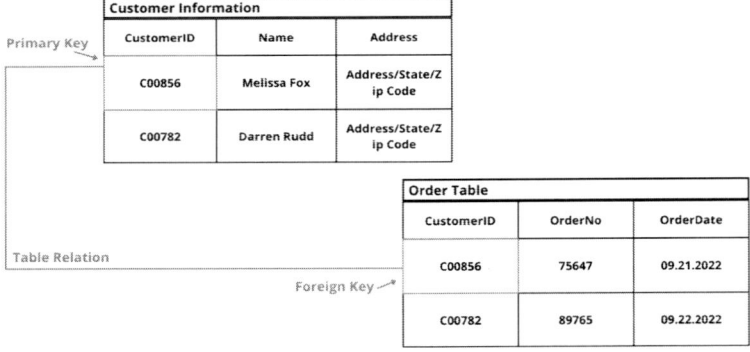

**FIGURE 5.1**

A great example would be company transactional data. There may be a table with customer information and separate tables with different transactions for different products. This could look something like a customer table (with customer information), orders table (with customer orders), and product tables (separating the different products.) Your query can then pull information from the separate tables simultaneously based on the specific information required. Customer 001, order #7754, product X.

**Customer Information**

| CustomerID | Name | Address |
|---|---|---|
| C00856 | Melissa Fox | Address/State/Zip Code |
| C00782 | Darren Rudd | Address/State/Zip Code |
| C00556 | Luna Ellis | Address/State/Zip Code |

**Customer Orders**

| CustomerID | OrderNo | ShipAddress |
|---|---|---|
| C00856 | 75647 | Address/State/ZipCode |
| C00782 | 89765 | Address/State/ZipCode |
| C00556 | 44563 | Address/State/ZipCode |

**Product Details**

| OrderNo | Product X Quantity | Product Y Quantity |
|---|---|---|
| 75647 | 02 | 0 |
| 89765 | 01 | 02 |
| 44563 | 0 | 01 |

1.Access Database

2. Create Query
Include X In Query

Customer information ⌐ X — CustomerID — T Customer Name — T

Customer Orders ⌐ — CustomerID — T X OrderNo — T

Product Details ⌐ — OrderNo — T X Product X Quan. — T X Product Y Quan. — T

3.End Result →

**Requested Query Used for Analysis**

| CustomerID | OrderNo | Product x Quantity | Product y Quantity |
|---|---|---|---|
| C00856 | 75647 | 02 | 0 |
| C00782 | 89765 | 01 | 02 |
| C00556 | 44563 | 0 | 01 |

**FIGURE 5.2** Relational database query example

## Hierarchical Database

This database management system is so named because it resembles the traditional hierarchy where items are ranked above others. There is a primary source of data called a parent or owner in the data-related context. It forms one-to-many relationships with other data sources that will be integrated into this data management system. As a result, all other data items integrated into this architecture will be related to the parent in some way or the other.

This system is used in very specific instances. For example, data may need to be connected and thus, analyzed about sea creatures. Sea creatures would be the parent data item, and other data items like saltwater and freshwater would be linked to the parent. Saltwater and freshwater would both have items linked underneath them. This would ultimately create a structure that looks like a tree. This differs from relational databases because relational database tables must be manually connected using keys, while hierarchical is all connected.

The data items need to be defined prior to gathering information for this system to work. Being at the top of this system, the parent and the items directly linked to the parent are easy to access and update.

The system has a few downsides. Relationships other than that with their parents are not allowed. Also, the lower down items come on the system, the harder they are to access or update. The fact that there can only be one parent can also serve as a disadvantage.

## Network Database

This system is more flexible than a hierarchy model, even though there are similarities between the two systems. The network system has a tree-like formation, but multiple parents can be integrated instead of just a single parent. Also, many-to-many relationships are allowed in such a system. This makes the system easier to navigate as information is easy to look up, no matter where it is linked or the type of relationship to other items.

The downside to using this type of system is the same thing that makes it beautiful. There are so many relationships that can be formed in multiple directions, which causes complexity to arise. As such, updates are tricky to perform as manipulating one data point can lead to changes across the board.

## Data Warehouses

A data warehouse is a relational database solely meant to perform queries and analyses. They often contain large amounts of historical data. It is stored in an extract, transform, and load process (ETL). This means information is extracted from its origin, transformed into high-quality data, then loaded into the warehouse ready for analysis. Data warehouses are ideal for online analytical processing (OLAP), allowing users to perform multi-dimensional analysis on high volumes of data.

## Data Lakes

Data lakes are another way to store unstructured data. While data warehouses are usually built on relational databases and only comprise of structured data, data lakes are generally home to a vast amount of structured, semi-structured, and unstructured data. Data lakes can be created in the cloud or on-premise with in-house data storage capabilities. Typically, data warehouses store data in hierarchical dimensions and tables, while a data lake uses a flat architecture to store data, mainly in files or object storage.

## Cloud Data Storage

Small and medium-sized businesses and organizations often use this method of data storage because of its inexpensive nature. No investment in expensive equipment is necessary as the data is stored on a cloud service. A cloud service is a solution that provides a remote network of servers hosted on the internet for the intended purpose of storing, managing, and processing data. The servers used in this type of data storage are not owned or managed by the data owners. Instead, they belong to the company that provides the cloud service. Because the data owners have handed over full responsibility of data storage to another entity, the cost for storing that data becomes much less. None of the equipment, special software, housing, or other infrastructure needs to be purchased. These benefits come at a predictable premium that the data owner is obliged to pay to continue using the service.

There are other benefits apart from the lowered cost of using a cloud service. One of these is that the solution is quite easily scalable. If the business or organization needs more storage space, it is simply a matter of paying an increased premium or switching service providers.

No MATTER THE type of data storage or storage devices used, the importance of data storage remains and one needs to be picked.

Luckily, the future for data storage is bright as demand grows in keeping with the growth of data that is always being created. After all, it is expected that the digital data created by businesses and organizations all around this green and blue ball that we live on will exceed 160 zettabytes. The capacity to store and manage this data needs to be in place before that time arrives. Who knows? Maybe, in the future, there may be an option that does not mean having to choose between cost, security, or smooth authorized accessibility to stored data.

# 6
# CLEANING YOUR DATA

"No data is clean, but most is useful."

— DEAN ABBOTT

The results you gain from using data are only as good as the quality of data that you use in the pursuit of achieving your goal. If your data metaphorically resembles a dump site, you will get garbage results. On the other hand, if you use high quality data, your result will also favor that characteristic. Good data always outweighs fancy algorithms.

Think of it as keeping up our health, with a little exercise, a clean diet, plenty of water, you'll be functioning great. Data needs to be treated with the same determination to keep up its good health. This chapter is about showing you how to get off on the right foot so that you not only begin the data sourcing process in a way that allows for sourcing as many bytes of clean data as possible. It also depicts how you can take data that has already been through the wringer and bring it up to that pristine quality. Good quality data equals good-quality decision-making, after all.

## What is Data Cleaning?

No data gathering procedure produces data that is 100% clean. The more data being collected or sourced, the higher percentage of data that will need to be put through the cleaning cycle. This is why it is important to double-check and triple-check data before using it. This checking process is also called data cleaning.

Data cleaning is a process that entails procedures that correct or remove corrupt, mislabeled, poorly formatted, duplicate, or incomplete data items within the data set as a whole. Data cleaning might seem boring to some, but don't be fooled. Better data quality means better insights, better decisions, more profits, and more promotions for the one managing the data.

The higher the quality of the data, the more valuable it becomes. Making decisions based on poor quality data typically leads to an unfavorable outcome. The last thing you want is for a group of executives to point out your analysis flaws because you didn't clean the data correctly. Or even worse, they trust you and make crucial decisions based on your discovery that may be slightly off. A very costly mistake you don't want to be a part of.

However, decision-making grounded on good quality data more than likely leads to increased productivity, faster results, more efficient operations, and access to greater resources, which are all conditions that allow businesses and organizations to thrive.

This leads to the benefits of this high-quality data:

- Better informed decision-making.
- Boosts results and revenue
- Saves money

- Saves time and increases productivity
- Gives companies a competitive advantage

## The 6 Characteristics of Good Data

How are you supposed to clean your data if you don't know what good data looks like? Understanding The 6 characteristics of good data is crucial, let's go through them:

## Accuracy and Precision

The first characteristic of good data is that it needs to be accurate and precise and as close to true values as possible. This means ensuring the sources are credible if you're sourcing secondary data and ensuring the data your company has collected is accurate based on the parameters set.

## Legitimacy and Validity

Remember, there are parameters set during the data collection process so that only data that falls within those confines are collected. Clean data adheres to these rules and ensures that the information is valid for use and achieving the ultimate goal of collecting that data. For example, if there are parameters for collecting data about a particular bee species, including the bees' size, color and flying habits within a certain area. Then including information about a separate bee species in that area would be invalid and thus hinder achieving the goal of collecting that data.

It is also essential to consider how the data obey these constraints and rules. This is to limit the type of data that can go into a table to ensure the values are accurate and consistent. Constraints can be column level or table level. Some constraints are:

- **Unique Constraint:** All values in a column or field are different across a dataset.
- **Mandatory Constraint:** Specific columns cannot be empty

- **Set-Membership Constraints:** Column values must be enum values. E.g., Predefined constants such as NORTH, SOUTH, EAST, or WEST.
- **Range Constraints:** Dates and numbers should generally fall within a specified range.
- **Data-Type Constraints:** Values must be of a particular data type. E.g., numeric, date.
- **Expression Patterns:** Text that must be a specific pattern, e.g., date formats, may be required to be mm/dd/yyyy
- **Foreign Key:** This enforces referential integrity. If a column value X refers to column value Y, then column value Y must exist—reference *relational databases* in the previous chapter for a refresher on keys.

Making sure your data confines to these parameters ensures that it can be accessed properly and run through algorithms without errors.

## RELIABILITY AND CONSISTENCY

In a perfect world, data would be collected from one source so that time and effort would be conserved and so that the results would be consistent across the board. However, we do not live in a perfect world and data often needs to be collected from different sources to gain a complete picture. As a result, there need to be systems in place to ensure that data collected from differing sources do not conflict with each other. For example, having data collected in different measurements such as inches vs centimeters can lead to inconsistent results. Cleaner data does not have inconsistencies.

## Timeliness and Relevance

The time at which data is collected is also relevant to how useful it is and therefore, how clean it is. For example, if the information is being collected about current fashion trends, collecting data about the future wants of consumers can lead to having information that is not valid. Data needs to be collected at the right time to ensure proper usefulness.

## Completeness and Comprehensiveness

If you thought using incorrect information was bad, you have never encountered the situation of using incomplete data. Having unfilled fields leads to a skewed view of what this data conveys. As a result, decision-making is flawed. A lot of the time, the algorithms you use will cause an error and won't be able to analyze data with missing values.

## Granularity and Uniqueness

The purpose of the collection of data will determine how detailed it needs to be. However, having too much detail or too little detail can lead to problems of confusion and inaccuracy. Clean data has the appropriate level of depth for the intended purpose.

## How to Clean Data (Data Scrubbing)

Let's say that your data does not have these 6 qualities. Not all is lost. Inaccurate, incomplete, and inconsistent data can be cleaned using the following steps:

## Remove Duplicate or Irrelevant Observations

This step involves removing data items that do not fall within the parameters set for the data collected as well as items that are duplicated across the set. Irrelevant and duplicate items are often a problem faced when data is collected from multiple sources. Taking the time to remove these duplicate or irrelevant items saves data analysts time and energy during the analysis process. Before removing duplicates, always copy your original data to another worksheet, so you don't accidentally delete important insights.

To filter for unique values in Excel: Click Data > Sort & Filter > Advanced

To remove duplicates in Excel: Click Data > Remove Duplicates, and then Under Columns, check or uncheck the columns where you want to remove the duplicates. In some instances, you might need all values. E.g., there might be $0.00 in sales for multiple products in February. Although duplicates are in the column, you wouldn't want to remove them as they are all relevant information to the analysis.

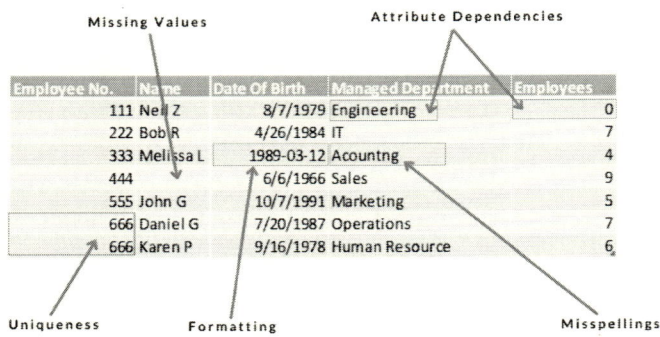

**FIGURE 6.1**

## Syntax Errors

Syntax: "the arrangement of words and phrases to create well-formed sentences in a language."

A syntax error is an error in the syntax of a sequence of characters, some examples are:

- **Typos:** A string (any series of characters that are interpreted literally by a script, e.g., "Norway," "66HKLZ8") can usually have many different abbreviations that are all necessarily correct but will cause an error if not formatted to be the same. E.g.,

Gender:

Male

M

Female

Fem.

F

- **Pad Strings:** Strings are generally padded in some way or the other. E.g., numerical codes usually need to be the same number of digits, so 488 would be 000488, if the string has six digits.
- **Remove spaces:** Remove unwanted spaces " November " > "November"

## Structural Errors

Not only are you spotting the typos, but ensuring each value is in a standardized format.

This includes:

- ensuring the values are either upper or lowercase in all strings.
- Make sure measurement units for numerical values stay consistent (cm to inches, etc.)
- Ensure dates are in the correct format based on company specifications and location (the US will have a different format than Europe.) To simplify, just keep everything consistent.

## Filter Unwanted Outliers

An outlier is a data item that differs from the rest of the set. More often than not, an outlier is a one-time observation that does not fit particularly well with the rest of the data set. Of course, there are times when this one-off observation is valid, but if it is not valid for achieving the goal of the data collection, it needs to be removed so that it does not impede the analysis process. Remember though that outliers are not necessarily incorrect so there needs to be a thorough consideration process as to whether or not the outlier should be kept or removed.

A simple way to find outliers is through data visualization. Once the data becomes visual, it will be evident if any points are out of place. Some effective visualizations to use:

Box plot: A box plot defines outliers as a data point located outside the whiskers of the box plot. It sets parameters based on the data and considers anything over or under the determined values, an outlier, making it very easy to spot them (we will learn more about the characteristics of a box plot in Chapter 10.)

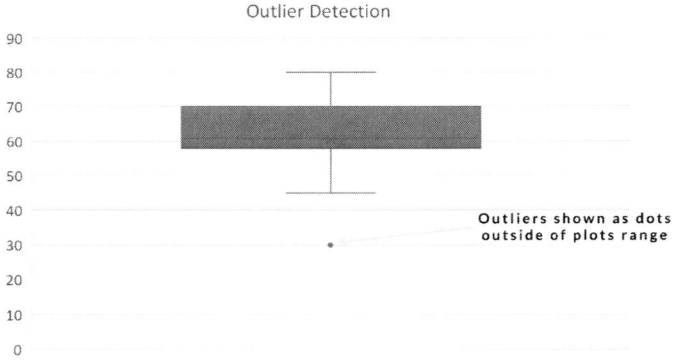

**FIGURE 6.2** Outlier detection with a box plot

Scatter plot: Scatter plots can also be useful to spot outliers. Keep in mind that scatter plots can also make it a bit more challenging to distinguish what is an outlier and what is just a high value, so make sure you double-check specific points so you're not removing key values.

There are some more advanced ways to remove outliers, such as interquartile ranges or standard deviation, but these methods are a bit out of reach for this book. Feel free to look into them if you get the chance.

**Handle Missing Data**

Remember that having incomplete data sets is just as bad or even worse than having incorrect data. This needs to be corrected immediately, and there are three options for doing so.

The first option is to simply discard data items that have missing values. However, this needs to be done mindfully as this may create holes in your data set as a whole. So, ensure that the data item is unnecessary for the analysis process before discarding it.

The second option is to conduct further data collection to input the missing values.

The third option is to flag it for the algorithm to know about. The missing value might have significance to your analysis. Do this with a "0" for numeric values or "missing" for categorical data. E.g., the same question in a given survey could have been skipped by multiple candidates. Why was it skipped?

It is essential to note the terminology used for incomplete values to correct them. E.g., Values like "0", "NA", "Null", "Not applicable", or "None", can all mean the same thing. The value is missing.

**Validation**

The final step of the clean-up process is to indeed ensure that the data is valid for use. This involves asking a few questions that need to be ticked off before sending this data for analysis. These questions include:

- Is this data logically sound?
- Does the data follow the rules set by the parameters in the initial collection process?
- Does the data bring any insight to light?
- Does the data support achieving the ultimate goal for its collection?
- Are there any trends developed from the data collected?

If the answer to any of these questions is not satisfactory then you need to restart the clean-up process. You need to do so until the data achieves the appropriate cleanliness that is fit for its use in the data's analysis.

## Data Transformation Techniques

After the data is clean, you can do a few things to make the data more readable for algorithms and analysis to gain more information. These include:

data binning/bucketing. Binning is used to reduce the effects of minor observational errors. It is a way to group data into smaller variables such as "bins" to be understood more effectively by algorithms and analysis. An example of this would be compiling ages into categories such as "10-20, 21-30, 31-40." Another example would be changing dates into desired categories such as "90s, 80s, 70s" or "March, April, May."

| Name | Date Of Birth |
|------|---------------|
| Neil Z | 8/7/1979 |
| Bob R | 4/26/1984 |
| Melissa L | 3/12/1989 |
| Alex M | 6/6/1966 |
| John G | 10/7/1991 |
| Daniel G | 7/20/1987 |
| Karen P | 9/16/1978 |

| Name | Date Of Birth |
|------|---------------|
| Neil Z | 70's |
| Bob R | 80's |
| Melissa L | 80's |
| Alex M | 60's |
| John G | 90's |
| Daniel G | 80's |
| Karen P | 70's |

**FIGURE 6.3**

Indicator Variables: This transforms categorical data into boolean values. For example, we can transform Male and Female into "o" and "1". This can be read easier by algorithms.

| Name | Gender | | Name | Is Female? |
|------|--------|---|------|-----------|
| Neil Z | M | → | Neil Z | 0 |
| Bob R | M | | Bob R | 0 |
| Melissa L | F | | Melissa L | 1 |
| Alex M | F | → | Alex M | 1 |
| John G | M | | John G | 0 |
| Daniel G | M | | Daniel G | 0 |
| Karen P | F | → | Karen P | 1 |

**FIGURE 6.4**

Grouping Outliers: When you have a variety of outliers, you can categorize them as one. Such as "Others" which makes for less clutter and cleaner analysis.

| Name | Country | | Name | Country |
|---|---|---|---|---|
| Neil Z | United States | → | Neil Z | United States |
| Bob R | United States | | Bob R | United States |
| Melissa L | United States | → | Melissa L | United States |
| Alex M | United States | | Alex M | United States |
| John G | United States | → | John G | United States |
| Daniel G | United Kingdom | | Daniel G | Other |
| Karen P | Canada | → | Karen P | Other |

**FIGURE 6.5**

## TOP 7 DATA CLEANING TOOLS

Cleaning data can be a tedious process. Many tools exist in this day and age to help you remove inconsistencies and inaccuracies as well as fill in incomplete items. An entire book can be written on this, but I will give you a brief rundown of some of the most popular and efficient data cleaning tools. Feel free to research some on your own and expand your knowledge. I also recommend learning SQL and Python, as they are essential for data cleaning and data analytics in general. Most business professionals will work in Excel, which is also capable of cleaning data. Some other applications include:

### OpenRefine

Formerly going by GoogleRefine, this powerful data cleaning software allows you to transform data from one format into another and clean the data. Some of the advantages of using this particular software are that it is open source and free to use, which translates into zero cost to you and constant updates by developers to make the software better. It also allows for sharing and collaborating during the process.

### Trifacta Wrangler

This is a cloud-based platform that allows for data cleaning—because of this, sharing and collaborating during the clean-up process is easy. Being a cloud platform makes easy access for multiple people and fast work for larger projects. However, this does come at a cost, as the platform is not free to use.

### Winpure Clean and Match

This software, like OpenRefine, boasts features like enhancing data quality by de-duplication, matching items to ensure consistency and cleansing information. It is also user-friendly without a steep learning curve. Unlike OpenRefine, though, its robust features come at a cost.

### TIBCO Clarity

This tool comes with additional features like data collection and data profiling. This could be the solution for you if you want more out of your data cleaning tool apart from its cleaning features.

### Melissa Clean Suite

This data cleaning tool claims to fight "dirty data" by verifying, correcting, amending and improving the consistency of data records. This cleaning tool is created to help sales teams and best serve customer relationship management (CRM) information.

### IBM Infosphere

This highly robust tool is especially useful for cleaning heterogeneous data. Heterogeneous data are records that are highly variable in format and structure. This makes it highly probable that there will be incomplete items, duplication and inaccuracy.

Therefore, if you have a high volume of data collected from several sources, this just might be the tool for you.

## Data Ladder

This data cleaning tool is most suitable for larger businesses and IT users with larger volumes of data that need to be cleaned.

## Excel

If you're like many business professionals and find yourself in Excel daily, a lot of your data cleaning needs can be filled within the software. Familiarizing yourself with the relevant commands will make it that much easier. Not everyone needs to access large databases and sift through terabytes of data. Assessing your day-to-day needs is essential to finding the most efficient process for your needs.

As I mentioned before, all of these data cleaning tools are great in their own right. I would recommend that you do a bit further research on each one - and others - to find which one best suits your criteria and will help you accomplish your specific goals.

# 7
# ANALYZING DATA

---

"Data is a tool for enhancing intuition."

— HILARY MASON

---

Your data is now squeaky clean. So, what do you do with it now? You use it to come up with conclusions that will align with your goals. Think of any lightbulb moment and you will know what I mean. But how does this happen? This chapter is the explanation that shows how data is used to gain insights.

Data is made to be presented to others. There would be no point to its collection if that was not true. The issue that arises is that it needs to be translated to most audiences for that purpose to come to fruition. That translation comes in the form of charts and graphs called data visualization. Data visualizations build a story so that audience can have a narrative to anchor them to what the data is conveying. Remember that lines of values and raw data generally incite headaches, but when that data is simplified with lines on a graph or sections of a bar chart, head-nodding to indicate understanding is more commonplace.

However, to meet that ultimatum of presentation, the data needs to be analyzed to present something coherent and educational. That is where analyzing the data that has been collected and cleaned is a necessary step. The first thing that needs to be understood is the different ways that you can approach data analysis. That approach defines what conclusions you will reach and ultimately how that data will be presented. We briefly looked at these data analysis types in chapter one, but the section below will take a deeper dive.

## TYPES OF DATA ANALYSIS

### Descriptive Analysis- "What Happened"

This is the simplest form of data analysis that any data analyst will come across. Does this method seek to provide the answer to *what happened?* The focus during data collection is on information about the past. There are two data-intensive processes highlighted in this method of data analysis. First comes data aggregation, which is the process of first gathering data and then presenting it in a summarized format so that the notable points are highlighted.

Once this application has taken place, then we move on to data mining. Data mining is the process that involves scanning large databases to pinpoint and gather specific data items so that new information can be derived from that stored collection by noting relationships and patterns between these data points. There are different techniques used to locate those specific data points, as the use of the word 'large' to describe these databases is by no means an exaggeration.

These techniques include:

- Classification analysis

- Clustering analysis
- Regression analysis
- Outlier detection
- Associated rules

We will go deeper into understanding these techniques in the following chapter. No matter the method used, this historical data will be analyzed to find and highlight trends and draw conclusions about what is likely to happen in the present or the future. One of the most classic uses of descriptive analysis is to track how a business is performing and thus, how actions like marketing and product development can be fine-tuned to build on past performance. Monthly revenue reports and sales lead overviews are examples of descriptive analysis.

## Diagnostic Analysis - "Why did this happen."

Data professionals do not have to limit themselves to only one type of analysis. After using descriptive analysis to find out what happened in the past, the data analyst can build on this by asking *why* it happened—the question of why is answered through the use of diagnostic analysis.

Diagnostic analysis builds on the insights gained from descriptive analysis to drill down on causation. Finding the cause of data's existence is just as important as the data itself. For example, a business may note historic steady growth in sales of a particular product over the last five years. Of course, the news of this development is excellent but understanding why can allow the business to leverage that performance to increase it even more.

Diagnostic analysis is particularly useful when outliers appear during the data collection process. Unfortunately, anomalies often mean a negative impact on businesses and organizations. Understanding the cause of why these anomalies arose in the first place puts companies and organizations in a position where they can adequately address these issues rather than putting a band-aid over them with only short-term solutions or, worse yet, guessing at how this should be fixed.

One of the biggest benefits of performing diagnostic analysis is that it allows you to be prepared in case the same problem or a similar problem arises in the future. It prompts the gathering of detailed information about the problem. Having that information already at hand is cost-effective and great for time management when future problems arise. Diagnostic analysis can be done manually, using an algorithm, or with statistical software (such as Microsoft Excel)

## Predictive Analysis - "What might happen in the future."

As the name hints, predictive analysis answers what is most likely to happen in the future. This type of analysis builds on the techniques used in descriptive and diagnostic analysis. The effectiveness of predictive analysis relies on a high-quality descriptive analysis, followed by the large amounts of data that would have been collected as a result of the diagnostic analysis.

Predictive analysis is not as commonly used as descriptive or diagnostic analysis. Rather, predictive analysis often comes in handy when a business or organization is facing difficulty and needs to develop a solid plan on how to proceed so that this difficulty is nullified most effectively. Risk analysis, such as those used by insurance companies, is a commonly referenced example of predictive analysis. Other examples of predictive analysis at work include analytics reports highlighting predictions about customer behavior in response to the release of a new product and sales forecasting.

## Prescriptive Analysis - "What should we do next."

Prescriptive analysis is a combination of all the other above-described types of analysis. It considers what happened, why it happened, and how problems can be fixed so that decision-making is effective at present and in the future. Whereas the other types of analysis are more heavily focused on monitoring data, this analysis process is more action-oriented. It uses the insights provided by the data monitoring in descriptive, diagnostic, and predictive analysis to implement solutions and strategies.

Prescriptive analysis is commonly used in science and mathematics communities. Artificial intelligence (AI) is the product of prescriptive analysis. The system that drives artificial intelligence uses large amounts of data to continuously learn and adapt so that this information is used to make more educated decisions. AI systems use these decisions to develop actionable plans.

As technology grows and provides more and more data, these systems become more adaptable and more advanced. This is why data-driven companies like Facebook and Apple are making such huge strides currently and are projected to bring bigger and better things to the table in the future.

As can be seen, these types of analysis have an interdependent relationship. As such, no one type of analysis should be disregarded by data analysts. They all bring something unique to the table and serve different purposes, but none of the insights are less valuable. While predictive analysis and prescriptive analysis require a little more technical know-how than descriptive analysis and diagnostic analysis, they should not be disregarded by any business or organization, as the solutions and actionable steps derived from them are invaluable. The value of descriptive and diagnostic analysis should not be discounted either, as predictive and prescriptive analysis cannot occur without their existence.

# 8
# DATA MINING AND MACHINE LEARNING ALGORITHMS

---

"If you torture the data long enough, it will confess to anything."

— RONALD COASE

---

I t is interesting to note that one of the biggest, real-world examples of machine learning is something that billions of people on this planet use on a daily basis. The social media platform Facebook is that example. Facebook uses a variety of algorithms that allow the platform to analyze user behavior and make recommendations for what articles and posts will appear on each user's feed. Other familiar examples include the recommendation systems that power websites like Spotify and Netflix, search engines like Google, and voice assistants like Alexa and Siri. These applications can only work as well as they do by collecting data about users. The engine drives these applications to use that data to make predictions about what you want to view in the future or what words best match the decibels you emit in the case of Siri and Alexa. Although machine learning and data mining can both be essential to a company's success with its data, understanding what makes them unique is critical.

## Data mining

Data mining is the process of searching, extracting, and analyzing a large amount of data to gain valuable insights and uncover trends about that data. This leads to more effective marketing strategies, increased sales, decreased costs, and many other benefits. Data mining is a tool that is used and monitored by humans.

## Machine learning

Meanwhile, machine learning is a method that automates analytical model building. The use of algorithms allows for the learning, identifying of patterns, and decision-making with minimal human involvement. Essentially an automated version of data mining. Not only is machine learning responsible for making your online activities as enjoyable as possible, but it is responsible for the majority of artificial intelligence developments that will come across your news feed. While such technology can seem unrelated to some people, artificial intelligence, Facebook, and Alexa all have a common ground: the use of machine learning technology that drives the systems to find and repeat patterns.

## Understanding The Difference

Data mining and machine learning are both a subset of data science, making the terms often interchangeable in many instances. Both processes utilize the same essential algorithms for discovering data insights and patterns, but their end result ultimately differs. Simply put, there are 2 main differences between the two:

1. Purpose: data mining is used to determine an outcome from an existing data set. While machine learning trains systems to execute complex tasks and predict future outcomes based on preexisting data.

2. Human Factor: Data mining relies on human interaction and is repeated constantly to gather insights from data. However, the main purpose of machine learning is to teach itself and not rely on any human influence. After the initial algorithms are set up, machine learning will continue to work independently. While data mining will need consistent interaction.

## Deep Learning

Deep learning is a technology that gives machines the ability to find and enhance those patterns. This technique of detection and amplification is known as a deep neural network. The word 'deep' describes how many layers of computation go into detecting and amplifying even the smallest patterns. This technique uses past data to predict the future.

The neural networks that power deep learning are reminiscent of the way the human brain works. Every time we learn something new, our brains are wired to factor that learning into how we proceed with the future and make decisions. For example, suppose we fall because we stepped in a particularly muddy area. In that case, our brain becomes rewired to adjust our footing if we happen upon this terrain or similar terrain in the future. It is also trying to map out other paths that we can take that might be safer. The brain has used past information to make predictions about how we can best proceed in the future to avoid a problem or make life better.

The neural networks that power the deep learning technology work in much the same way as they continuously rewire themselves to adapt to the new information they receive.

## Supervised, Unsupervised and Reinforcement Learning

Deep learning, and thus machine learning, happens in three ways. They are supervised, unsupervised, and reinforcement learning. There can be many subsets of machine learning and algorithms, which can get quite confusing. Before diving deep into some essential algorithms and analysis, familiarize yourself with this graph to understand how they relate.

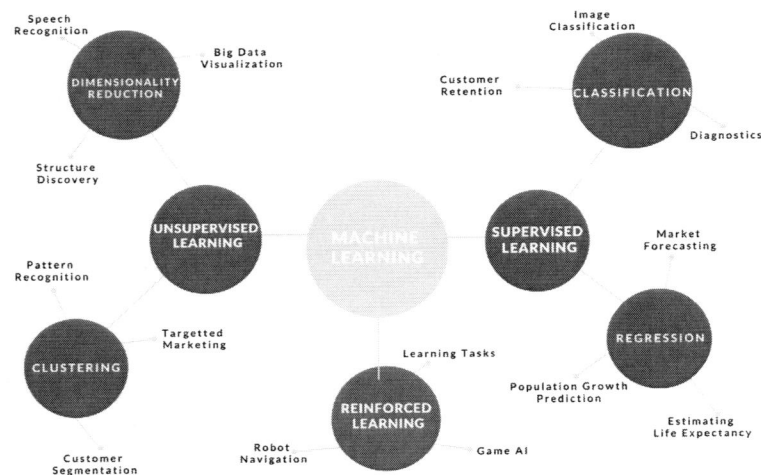

**FIGURE 8.1**

## SUPERVISED LEARNING

These algorithms are reliant on obtaining specific target outcomes based on rules that govern a given set of independent variables. It maps an input to an output based on example input-output pairs. The two main types of supervised learning are classification and regression. An example of supervised learning would be text classification. The goal is to predict the class label of a piece of text.

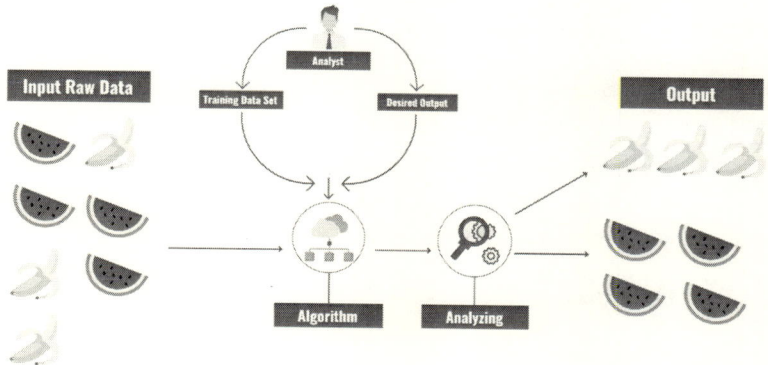

**FIGURE 8.2** Supervised Learning- **Goal:** Perform tasks as good as humans. **Task:** Clearly Defined (with desired output). **Training Data Set**: Yes

## Unsupervised Learning

Unsupervised learning uses machine learning algorithms to analyze and cluster unlabeled datasets. They can discover patterns and group similar items without any human involvement. It is known as "Unsupervised" as it doesn't have a training output to reference. The most common unsupervised learning tactic is known as "Clustering" which is used to group similar values in a data set.

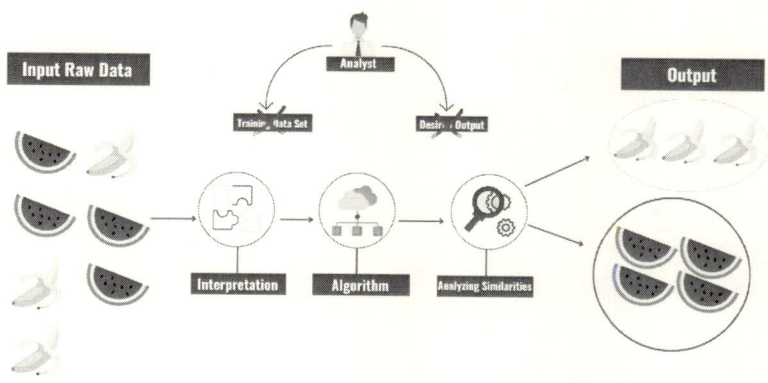

**FIGURE 8.3** Unsupervised Learning- **Goal:** To find structure in the data. **Task:** Vaguely Defined. **Training Data Set:** No

## Reinforcement Learning

Reinforcement learning is the most advanced out of the three. It trains machine learning models to learn in an interactive environment using trial and error feedback from its actions and experiences. In the simplest form, it takes action, fails, learns from the failure, and attempts to act correctly the next time. Although prominent in robotics and AI, it is a relatively new concept in data science. I'll keep reinforcement learning brief as it is a fairly advanced technique. We don't want to stray away from significant information for a method that you will rarely, if not ever, use until later in your career.

### TYPES OF ALGORITHMS

## Regression (Supervised Learning)

Regression analysis is the process of first identifying and then analyzing the relationship between the variables that may link or differentiate data items. This technique is instrumental in making predictions and forecasts as it allows whoever is working with the data to note how variables are dependent and interdependent. You're essentially trying to find a line or curve representing the patterns in the data. An example would be medical researchers often use linear regression to understand the relationship between drug dosage and blood pressure in patients. The researchers would administer several dosages of a particular drug to patients and observe their blood pressure response. With a simple regression model, they would use dosage as the predictor variable and blood pressure as the response variable. Some important regression algorithms to know are:

- Linear Regression

Linear regression predicts an outcome based on continuous features. It establishes a relationship between dependant and independent variables by fitting a "best line,", commonly called the regression line. The variable you are predicting is the dependent variable (aka the response variable.) The variable you are using to predict the value of that variable is called the independent variable (aka explanatory or predictor variable.) The simple formula to remember for a linear regression line is $Y = a + bX$.

Y is the Dependant variable (that represents the Y-axis,) and X is the independent variable (which is plotted on the X-axis.) "b" represents the slope line, thus determining its steepness, and the "a" is the intercept (value of "Y" when "X" = 0.) Let's look at an example. In this case, we are comparing advertising cost (independent variable) to the number of conversions (dependant variable.) Let's plot this data.

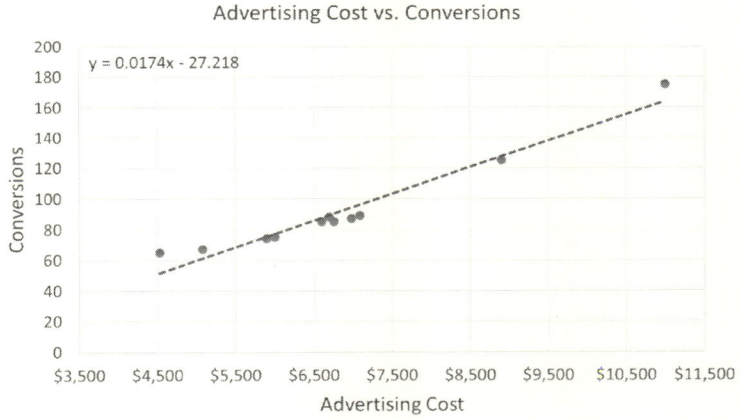

**FIGURE 8.4** Linear Regression

We have 12 data points to showcase the 12 months of the year, showing the ad spend and the number of conversions for each month. The given change in the independent variable determines the dependant variable's value. We can use the relationship between the independent and dependent variables to predict the trajectory of the data and conversion rate.

The goal of linear regression is to create a line that creates the least amount of distance between the points and the line, so it represents the true trajectory of the data.

- Non-linear Regression

When a set of data doesn't follow the rules of a linear model, then it is essentially a non-linear model. Nonlinear regression is similar to linear regression as it relates two variables (X and Y) just in a non-linear (curved) relationship.

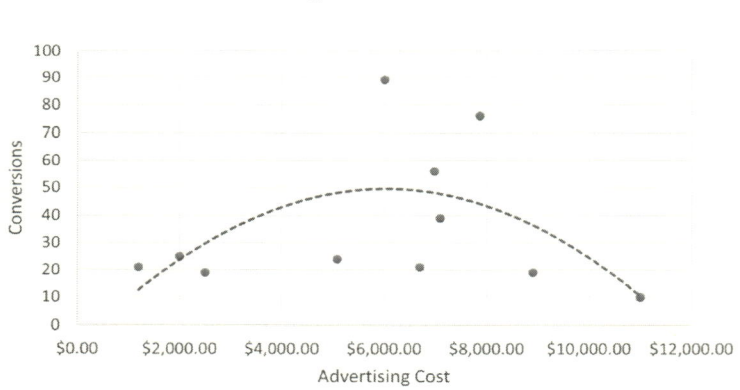

FIGURE 8.5 Non-linear regression

An example of this would be exponential regression. Exponential regression is the same concept as linear regression: finding a trajectory regression line that best fits the data. An extreme spike in the data makes it non-linear, rendering a linear regression line ineffective. The line is more of an exponential curve. An example of exponential data would be bacteria growth/decay, population growth/decline, or investment growth/decline. These data sets rapidly increase and decrease more significantly than a linear model.

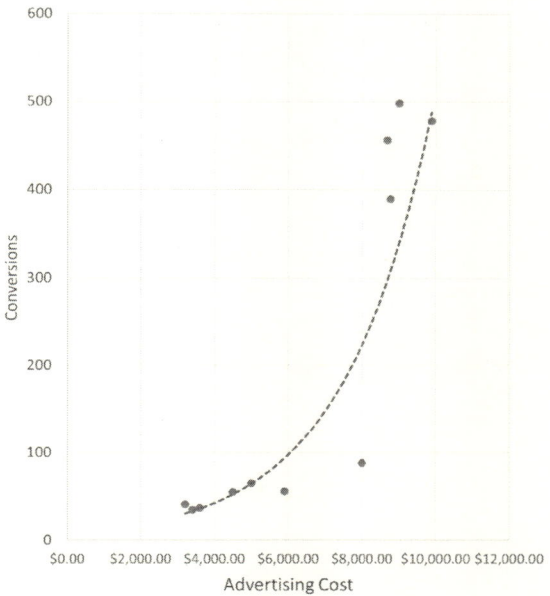

**FIGURE 8.6** Exponential regression

## Classification (Supervised Learning)

Classification is essentially an algorithm recognizing objects and categorizing them accordingly. It helps us separate vast quantities of data into discrete values. E.g., 0/1, True/False, or pre-determined output labels. Some important classification algorithms to know are:

- Logistic Regression

Logistic regression is used to estimate discrete binary values such as yes/no, true/false and 0/1 based on a set of independent variables. Essentially, it predicts the probability of the occurrence of an event by fitting the data into a logistic function or logistic curve.

For example, categorizing tests passed based on hours studied. Logistic regression fits an S-shaped logistic function instead of fitting a line to the data. The curve tells you the probability of passing a test, based on hours studied. If you have many hours studied, there is a high probability you will pass the test. If you have a medium amount of time spent studying, there is only a 50% chance you will pass the test. There's only a small probability you will pass the test if you have minimal hours studied. Although logistic regression determines a specific outcome, it is used for classification. For example, if the probability of passing the test is greater than 50% (based on hours studied), it will be classified as passed. If it is below 50%, it will be classified as failed.

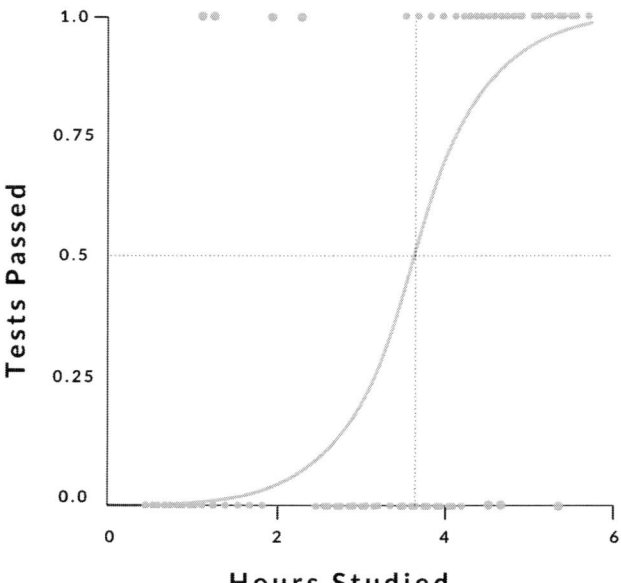

**FIGURE 8.7** Logistic regression

Based on this analysis, we can determine that the students who studied for more than 3.7 hours had a much higher rate of passing a test.

- Decision Trees

A decision tree is a type of supervised learning mainly used for classification problems. It works for both categorical and continuous input and output variables. It splits the sample into two or more sets based on the most significant splitter/differentiator in input values. This algorithm takes the entire data set and progressively places it in smaller groups. It differentiates these groups by specific features. Think of it as a tree with several branches coming from one stem. A simple example of this would be dictating if you will go on a hike based on the weather.

| Day | Outlook | Temperature | Humidity | Wind | Hike? |
|---|---|---|---|---|---|
| 1 | Sunny | Mild | Normal | Strong | Yes |
| 2 | Sunny | Hot | High | Strong | No |
| 3 | Overcast | Hot | High | Weak | Yes |
| 4 | Overcast | Mild | High | Strong | Yes |
| 5 | Rain | Cool | Normal | Weak | Yes |
| 6 | Rain | Mild | High | Strong | No |
| 7 | Overcast | Cool | Normal | Strong | Yes |
| 8 | Sunny | Mild | High | Weak | No |
| 9 | Sunny | Cool | Normal | Weak | Yes |
| 10 | Rain | Mild | Normal | Weak | Yes |
| 11 | Rain | Mild | High | Weak | Yes |
| 12 | Sunny | Hot | High | Weak | No |
| 13 | Overcast | Hot | Normal | Weak | Yes |
| 14 | Overcast | Hot | High | Strong | No |

**FIGURE 8.8**

# Should You Go For a Hike?

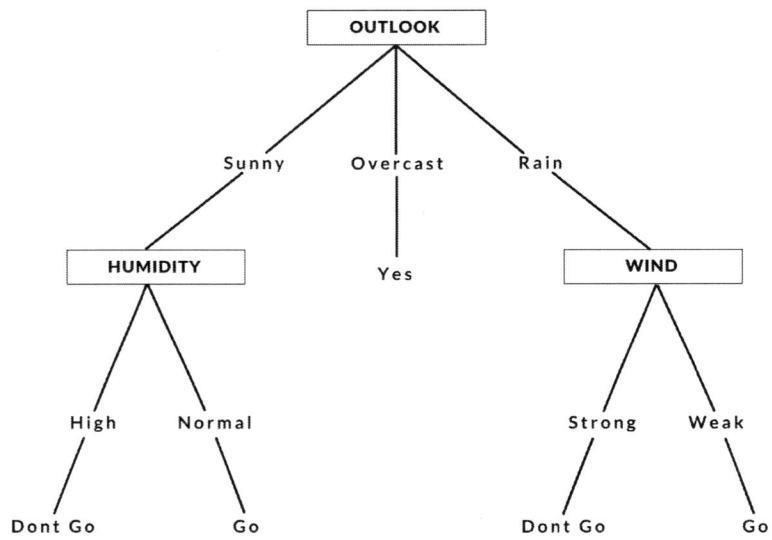

**FIGURE 8.9**

## CLUSTERING (UNSUPERVISED LEARNING)

A cluster is a collection of data that share similar qualities and thus, can be grouped based on these characteristics. This type of analysis is similar to classification, as data is placed in like groups. The difference is that classification derives these groups from predetermined characteristics. On the other hand, the groups derived from clustering develops without prior knowledge of grouping systems. They develop more organically. Let's go through some essential clustering algorithms.

- K-Means

K-means is a clustering algorithm responsible for finding group-ings within data. The number of groups is represented by the vari-able K. The algorithm repeatedly runs and assigns each data point to one of the K-groups based on their feature similarity. This repe-tition will continue until data items do not change the cluster they belong to. There are many instances where K-means can be extremely useful for a business. One good example would be during a new product launch. When it comes time for advertising campaigns, you can group customers into clusters based on similar interests and deliver a different advertisement to each group of people that matches their interests.

To begin the algorithm you start out by determining the value for K (amount of clusters) then select an initial centroid (center of each cluster.)

1. Assign each observation to its nearest centroid (cluster.)
2. Update the centroids to be the center of their new observations.
3. Repeat these steps until the data points cease to change clusters.

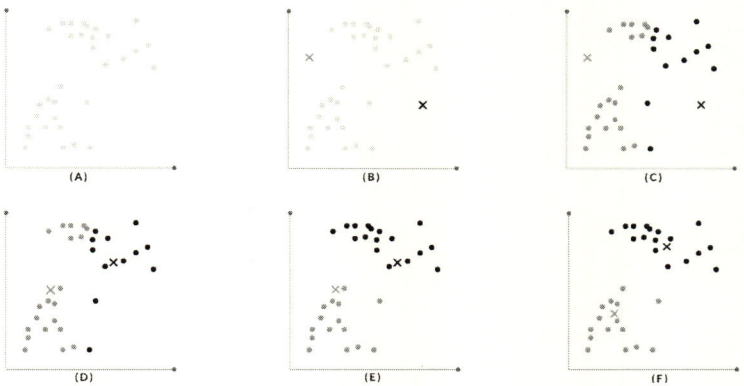

FIGURE 8.10

SOME MORE COMMON algorithms worth familiarizing yourself with over time:

• SVM Algorithm

SVM stands for Support Vector Machine. This type of algorithm is used to classify items in a data set by plotting particular variables of that dataset and linking those items based on those variable features. This supervised learning technique is mainly used for classification but can also be useful in regression analysis.

• Naive Bayes Algorithm

This particular algorithm comprises a family of smaller algorithms that share a particular rule whereby variables are interdependent. Based on this principle, finding a variable that does not belong is easy. This is a supervised learning technique.

• kNN Algorithm

kNN stands for k-nearest neighbor. This unsupervised machine learning algorithm is one used for classification by estimating how likely a data item is dependent on its nearest neighbor in that data set.

• Random Forest Algorithm

This is a supervised learning algorithm that makes use of several decision tree learning algorithms to classify data items. New data items are classified within particular trees based on how well it fits onto a 'branch' of that tree.

• Dimensionality Reduction Algorithms

This is an unsupervised learning technique. This particular algorithm aims to reduce the number of variables within a particular data set. It does this by reducing the number of variables. Reducing the number of pixels in a picture to make it smoother is an example of this particular algorithm at work.

- Gradient Boosting Algorithm

This algorithm is used when faced with large volumes of data. It uses data models and combines them to make an overall higher accurate prediction of what the next data model that will be included in the set will be. This is a supervised machine learning technique.

MANY OF THESE algorithms won't be useful until you are further into a data science career. If you are starting to get sweaty palms, don't fear, there are many career options available that don't require you to be well versed in this complex stuff day to day, like a business analyst. It's essential to have a clear roadmap of where you want to go (or at least an idea) to efficiently spend your time learning what's useful and avoiding what isn't. That leads us to our next chapter and a potential career field, business intelligence.

# 9
# BUSINESS INTELLIGENCE

---

"BI is about providing the right data at a the right time to the right people so that they can take the right decisions."

— NIC SMITH

---

In the world of data analytics, many companies utilize their gathered information to predict future outcomes and make better business decisions. Now, you're probably wondering why everyone is focused on the future and not on the "now," which inevitably creates the future. Well, that's where business intelligence comes in. Business intelligence (BI) provides insights into the current state of the business. BI is an integrated system that allows businesses to manage, track and analyze critical business information such as key performance indicators (KPIs,) financial statements, customer transactions, etc. Implementing BI allows essential metrics to be stored in one place, which many employees can access and analyze regardless of their technical background.

## BI vs. Data Analytics

It can be difficult to differentiate all of these terms while they're being thrown around. In its simplest form, BI is descriptive. It tells us what's happening now and what happened in the past to create our current state. Usually through company analytics and reports (sales reports, customer information, website traffic.) BI aims to deliver a precise picture of the current state of affairs to business executives. Data analytics, however, is predictive. It's the processing of raw data to predict future outcomes and decide what can be done to achieve or avoid those outcomes. It requires data scientists to analyze and interpret raw data.

Another defining characteristic of BI is that it can be a lot more user-friendly, as there is minimal technical analysis and a lower barrier to entry. BI tools have come to be very intuitive and user-friendly. Today, it is prevalent to have non-technical individuals use BI tools to produce reports based on their companies' metrics. Although having minimal knowledge in data analytics or modeling, many marketing, finance, and operations experts can rely on BI tools to give them the information and insights they need.

## BI Strategy

BI is generally a system that gets integrated into your business to track critical data—as with data analytics, having a strategy is essential to an efficient system. You want to create a clear roadmap for smooth integration into your business. There are many ways to approach a potential BI strategy. Let's look at a straightforward 4 step plan to get your feet wet.

**Step 1** - Get Input From Your Team

It is important you get input from various sources such as executives or managers to find out important details that may affect your BI system. Some details include who will be accessing the system? what specific tasks will it need to perform? What budget is available? What workloads will the software take over? As well as anything else that is relevant. An overlooked yet vital thing to consider is will the software be able to integrate into your current system without any modifications. You don't want to spend a large sum just to be at the same place you started because the tool doesn't work with your servers.

**Step 2** - Determine Goals for the System

Determining what exactly you want the system to deliver is a crucial task. You have to ask yourself and your team questions such as what insights you require from the system? What KPIs are essential to track? This will also help you determine other factors down the line, like what platform will be best for your business.

**Step 3** - Determine Your Budget

Most software comes with different bells and whistles, with varying prices. Determining a budget enables you to find the best system within your range. This also allows you to have any wiggle room for any extra costs down the line.

**Step 4** - Select a System

Now that you have the requirements, goals, and budget, you should be able to assess the multitude of software available and select the most efficient program to integrate into your system. From there, employees can track important data, create dashboards for visualization purposes, and monitor your business's metrics and KPIs.

## How BI Can Transform A Business

Implementing a BI strategy into your business is a proven way to maximize revenue and stay competitive. Let's walk through a few quick examples to gain a better understanding.

CASE STUDY #1

A biotech company needs to develop a more strategic marketing plan for the upcoming year. They want to increase market share and overall profits. Their company lacks processes and systems essential to capturing and analyzing customer data.

**Goal:** Uncover high-value customers and marketing opportunities.

**Problems:**

- They have no way of categorizing their customers based on key parameters for specific targeting.
- They have no marketing campaign analytics or ways to track their impact.
- They don't have an integrated data collection system.

**Possible solution:**

The company can implement a BI platform, which collects and integrates multiple metrics into a single place. They can calculate specific marketing metrics needed and segment the data for future targeted campaigns. Resulting in lower expenses, higher conversions and the discovery of high-value customers.

CASE STUDY #2

**New York Shipping Exchange (NYSHEX)**

New York Shipping Exchange is a shipping-technology company that improves shipping processes overseas.

**Goal:** Streamlining their data for easy access and analysis.

**Problems:** NYSHEX would manually extract data from its various locations and import it into Excel for data analysis. It was a labor-intensive project which rendered the data only accessible to a select few, causing the engineers to be overwhelmed with requests.

**Solution:** NYSHEX implemented BI, which centralized its data into one system while giving the entire company access. Even those with no technical experience could access, analyze and visualize the data. The company was able to triple its shipping volume between the United States and Asia in 2019.

WHATEVER BUSINESS REQUIREMENTS YOU HAVE, a BI system can drastically improve the effectiveness of your day-to-day operations. You can save time and money, create productive and happy employees, and gain a competitive edge over your competition.

# 10

# INTRODUCTION TO DATA VISUALIZATION

---

"The goal is to turn data into information, and information into insight."

— CARLY FIORINA

---

Your data is cleaned and analyzed to give you clear insights. However, this is only valuable to the data professional that brought it to light. It needs to be shared with the right people to make effective business decisions. This leads to data visualization.

If data was easy for everyone to understand, most people could claim to be data experts. However, data professionals are of an advanced skillset. They possess the ability to effectively translate data into understandable pieces of nuggets for other people to absorb.

Data translated into visualizations that others can understand is called data visualization. This chapter dives into exactly what data visualizations are and how we can use them effectively.

It's important to understand that even the best visuals won't make up for a poorly planned presentation. Knowing what information to present is essential for creating effective data visualizations. For example, let's say your team is about to launch a new product, and you're determining a price point. You've researched similar products and their pricing over the past five years and came up with a launch price based on the competitor average. You now have to present these findings to the product manager. Considering they already have a lot of in-depth knowledge of the product, presenting this might entail a simple line graph, showcasing similar product pricing over time while highlighting the average price of competitors and where the product should be priced. Now, If the product manager has to present why they selected this price point to the executives or even the CEO, They would have to be a little more in-depth—adding an additional graph showcasing the profit margins. This shows the executives that the price point is competitive, profitable and in alignment with company goals. It is crucial that you always consider your audience and what information they need, so you can avoid an unfinished presentation.

Let's look at a brief snippet from my book "How To Win With Your Data Visualizations" to get a better idea of what a good data story entails.

*"With the many, many bytes of information available for relating to other people, how do you decide which ones deserve precedence and should be added to your slides? That is a fundamental question when approaching data storytelling. If this question has come to your mind, you have set yourself up with the right mindset to present data in the most digestible way to your audience. The answer of which bytes of information you will relate to your audience depends on your final goal of the presentation. Too many business professionals get stuck on the visual aspects of the presentation and leave the information that needs to be relayed as an afterthought. But it is truly the other way around. The visuals do*

*not matter if your audience cannot follow a defined path from the initial insight to a solution.*

*A narrative is about developing a language that allows for augmenting data in the most effective way to deliver to an audience so that the people in the audience are not left confused and trying to piece together these bytes of information. The narrative is the vehicle that conveys insights on the data that has been collected to the audience. There are 3 main components of a great narrative. The what, The who, and the how.*

**The What:** *What is the goal of your presentation? What insights do you need to convey? What solutions do you need to guide your audience toward? The "what" is arguably the most important part of any data story. Without having a goal in mind, you will not know what insights to bring forward and how you will effectively present them.*

**The Who:** *Who are you presenting to? Knowing this is essential when presenting data because you need to know what they already know, and what they don't. What you present to your product manager vs. the CEO is very different. Finding out who you're presenting to will allow you to determine what you need to present and how you will present it. This will be covered more in-depth in chapter 2.*

**The How:** *Now that you know what you're presenting and who you're presenting it to, how you will do it should come naturally. Based on what you've already learned, you can select specific insights with supporting information and transmit them through beautifully crafted data visualizations in a favorable sequence. Of course, the bulk of the book shows you exactly how to do this, so I will not go any more in-depth here. Keep reading!"*

Scan the QR code below, or click the link (for kindle readers) if you'd like to check out "How To Win With Your Data Visualizations". It goes more in-depth with the presentation process and teaches you how to create visualizations that are effective and aesthetic. How To Win With Your Data Visualizations

## USE THE RIGHT VISUALS

Inputting the right visual for conveying data allows data professionals to take complex information and relay it in a simple form that is easy for people of all expertise levels to understand. There are many different types of data visualizations.

The first step in using data visuals to the fullest advantage is actually choosing the right visualization appropriate for the circumstance. That choice boils down to questions that you must ask yourself. Such questions include, what type of data are you trying to represent? Is it data that is part of a whole or different data sets? Is it data that shows the relationship between two or more data sets? The answers to these questions allow you to drill down on the type of data visualization that makes the most sense for that portrayal.

The four main categories of charts are:

### Comparison Charts

Comparison charts allow for the comparison of at least two sets of data. This comparison can either highlight the similarities or the differences between these data sets. Some of the best charts for making comparisons include bar charts, column charts, and line charts.

## Composition Charts

Composition charts allow for showcasing the different parts of one whole set of data and how these parts changed over time. Some of the best charts for portraying composition include pie charts, pyramids, stacked column charts and area charts.

## Relationship Charts

Relationship charts are used to show the connection between at least two variables in data sets. Some of the best data visualizations for portraying relationships between data sets include bubble charts and scatter plots.

## Distribution Charts

Distribution charts are used to identify trends and outliers by highlighting how variables are distributed over time. Some of the best charts for highlighting distribution include scatter plots, area charts and line graphs.

### TYPES OF CHARTS

Let's go through some important visualizations you can utilize:

**Infographics:** Sometimes, your boss or executives want a quick rundown of multiple KPIs in your company. This is where infographics come in handy. Infographics are used to showcase a lot of information quickly and clearly. They are ideal for showing the bigger picture of a lot of data instead of critical specific insights. If you've done extensive analysis to find some crucial insights, a single visualization per insight and a proper presentation might be a better option.

**FIGURE 10.1**

# Technology's Impact on Child Development

Recent surveys show that 85% of parents allow their young children access to technology: tablets, smartphones, televisions, and computers.

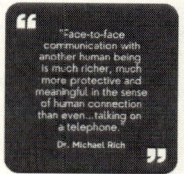

"Face-to-face communication with another human being is much richer, much more protective and meaningful in the sense of human connection than even...talking on a telephone."

Dr. Michael Rich

Children have more difficulty understanding sounds from devices such as smartphones and tablets as opposed to hearing the voice of an actual person trying to communicate.

**86%**

**Parents satisfied with technology's effect on their children.**

They associate their children's strong comprehension of literacy with tablet use.

**72%**

**Parents concerned with technology use.**

Screen time includes inappropriate content, affects sleep, and takes away from outdoor time.

**15%**

**Parents who do not allow screen time at home.**

There is zero access to devices and more outdoor time and face to face interaction is encouraged.

The duration of screen time is crucial in homes that allow children access to smartphones, tablets, televisions, and computers. Child development experts emphasize the importance of consciousness —that screen time should not replace what is most essential for child development: human interaction.

**FIGURE 10.2**

**Bar Graph:** Bar graphs, horizontal bar graphs and stacked bar graphs are all the tried and true visualization methods in business. They work great for comparing values like sales figures by month or website traffic by country—they're ideal for conveying quick and clear insights to your team.

**FIGURE 10.3**

**Line Graph:** Another common chart is a line graph, which are great for showcasing trends over time. Whether it's revenue for the year or housing prices over the last ten years. Line graphs are also useful for reviewing numbers, whether quarterly, yearly, or monthly, to monitor spikes and dips to better understand business performance.

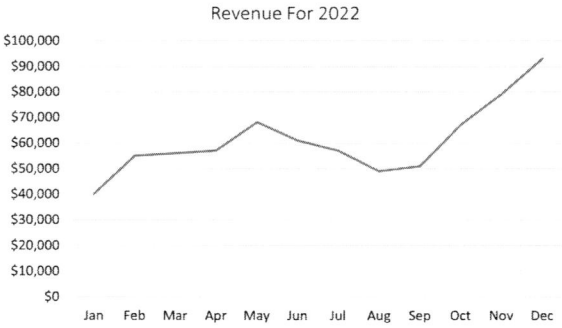

**FIGURE 10.4**

**Scatter Plot:** Scatter plots are used to display and compare values from two variables. Scatter plots are great because they report individual values, but when absorbed as a whole, you can spot patterns and trends. Identification of correlational relationships is a common practice for anyone using scatter plots. When given a particular horizontal value, we can adequately predict the vertical value. The horizontal axis is known as the independent variable, while the vertical axis is the dependent variable. Relationships between variables can come in many forms: positive or negative, strong or weak, linear or non-linear.

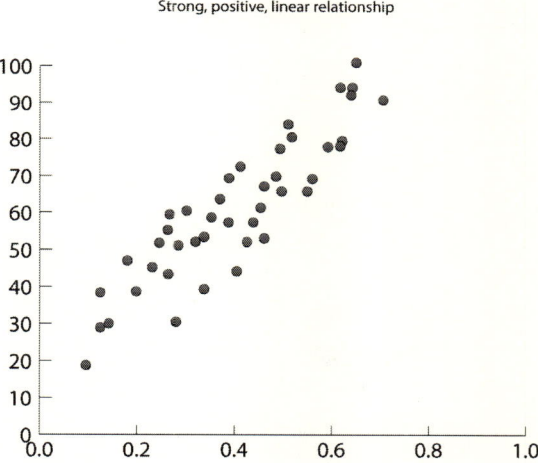

**FIGURE 10.5** Scatter plot

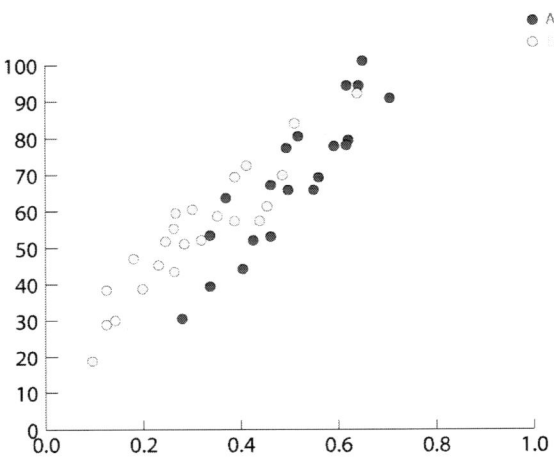

**FIGURE 10.6** Scatter plot comparing two variables

**Box Plot:** A box plot is a graphical rendition of statistical data. It is a standardized way of displaying the distribution of data based on a five-number summary minimum. First quartile, median value, third quartile and maximum value. With the "Mean" Value representing the average of the dataset. Essentially, it compares the distribution of a data set.

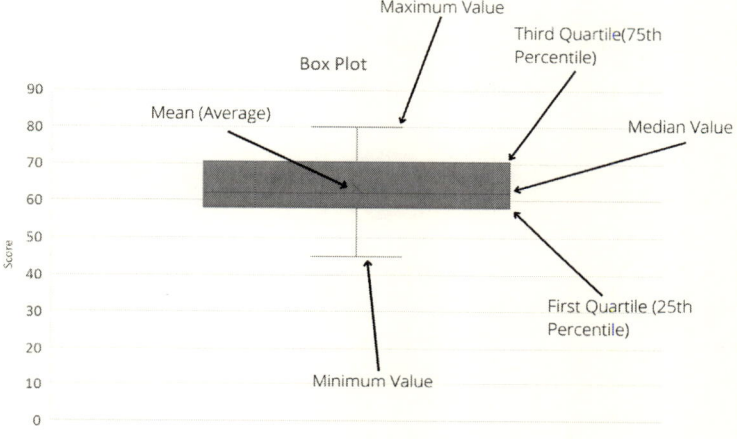

**FIGURE 10.7**

You can also compare data sets and their distribution.

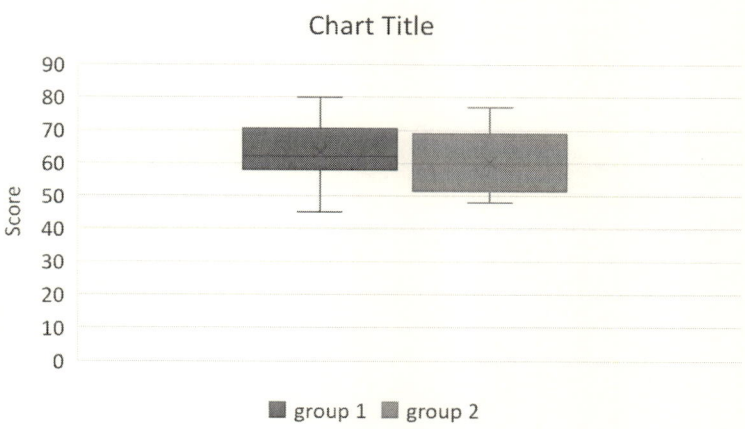

**FIGURE 10.8**

**Heat Map:** A heat map is a data visualization where a color represents the numerical figures of each value. A light color usually means less and dark color means more. This can also be referred to as a "sequential" color palette. A great example would be a map of America, showcasing the population of cities. The color will be very dark in high population areas and fade out as the population gets smaller. The same concept would apply to website traffic throughout the world. Heat Maps can also be helpful with a table that shows figures from multiple marketing campaigns over the years—highlighting which campaigns made the most revenue so you can easily spot the top performers. In this case, green would be showcasing the highest values, and red would showcase the lowest values, fading lighter or darker based on the value.

**FIGURE 10.9**

| | Q1 | Q2 | Q3 | Q4 |
|---|---|---|---|---|
| Campaign 1 | $50,000 | $85,000 | $75,000 | $98,000 |
| Campaign 2 | $75,000 | $79,000 | $65,000 | $86,000 |
| Campaign 3 | $100,000 | $110,000 | $90,000 | $125,000 |
| Campaign 4 | $56,000 | $59,000 | $50,000 | $67,000 |
| Campaign 5 | $43,000 | $69,000 | $60,000 | $65,000 |
| Campaign 6 | $78,000 | $70,000 | $77,000 | $82,000 |
| Campaign 7 | $68,000 | $67,000 | $60,000 | $77,000 |
| Campaign 8 | $55,000 | $50,000 | $56,000 | $62,000 |

**FIGURE 10.10**

Although there are a plethora of visualizations you can use, it's important to start with the essentials and not overwhelm yourself. These charts can cover almost all of your bases, but as you excel in your career, continue trying new methods to tell the most effective data stories.

Once you have chosen your particular visualization, it is time to get to the design phase. Some people are tempted to use bright, bold and colorful charts, but doing so will only serve to mislead or confuse the audience. Design must be approached carefully and should be clean, concise and clutter-free.

To ensure that your data visualizations are clutter-free, here are a few tips:

- Ensure that the chart is appropriately labeled and legible. Your audience should not have to squint to note what is labeled on your chart or have to scratch their head when they connect the dots.
- Do not use uppercase text unnecessarily. Just like adding big clunky furniture to a small space, uppercase letters will clutter your visualizations. Limit using uppercase text to instances where you are trying to call attention to a particular element on a chart or a title.

- Ensure that the charts are not misleading by doing any of the following:
- Omitting the baseline, which is the zero value at the vertical axis.
- Manipulating the y-axis with disproportionate scales.
- Cherry Picking favorable sets of data to highlight in your charts. All relevant data should be represented without bias.
- Using the wrong type of chart to display information, such as using a pie chart to highlight comparisons. (the information can easily get lost with all the slices being similar sizes. A horizontal bar chart would be better for this. Rank the values in order from highest to lowest.)
- Do not overuse bright, bold colors as they can detract from the message you send. When such colors are used, ensure that the use is relevant to bring attention to particular details on the chart.
- Do not use dark grid lines. Using gridlines is meant to make charts easier to read, but if they overpower the rest of the chart, that defeats the purpose of the use. When it is necessary to use gridlines, use soft grey ones but my advice is to eliminate their use when possible.

## DATA VISUALIZATION TOOLS

New data visualization software is coming out all the time. But there are a few dependable programs that won't be going anywhere anytime soon. My top 3 data visualization tools would be:

### Excel

Excel is widely known and used by many. It's also very user-friendly and easy to create beautiful visualizations. If you're the average business professional, writing quarterly reports and tracking metrics, Excel is all you'll ever need. It's very intuitive and can quickly turn a set of data into a chart and that chart into an engaging visual with some slight customization.

## Power BI

Power BI is the older brother of Excel. It has that extra processing power to work with larger sets of data. Their dashboards are also more interactive and customizable than those in excel. You can also argue they're prettier. Power BI excels in comparison between tables, reports, and data files. It's used prevalently in business intelligence, hence the BI.

Power BI is a fan favorite. It can connect to many different file data sources, including Excel and CSV, as well as database sources like Oracle, SQL Server, IBM and much more. It also makes it easy to export your reports as JPGs or PowerPoint slides, so you can seamlessly go from reporting to visualizing.

## Tableau

We are now at higher levels of data visualization. Tableau can visualize even the most extensive data sets without limitations on the number of data points or row size. It is faster and provides extensive features for visualizing data and creating intricate dashboards. When you want to visualize big data, Tableau will not fall short. Of course, the more elaborate the program, the higher the cost, which is a tradeoff.

## Python and R

I'll toss in a bonus option for any aspiring data science nerds. With the ability to code in Python or R, you also can create complex data visualizations. Python visualization libraries such as Matpoltlib or Seaborn allow you to turn your data into engaging, interactive charts with one line of code. If you plan to learn any of these languages, learning these skills is recommended.

By mastering these tools, you'll be set up to visualize any set of data, at any time. Pair that with some killer presentation skills, and you're well on your way to a fantastic career as a data or business professional.

We are only scratching the surface of data visualization in this book. If you'd like to go more in-depth, check out my first book, "How To Win With your Data Visualizations," I mentioned earlier, or join my email list at ElizabethSClarke.com for future updates on new projects and content.

# 11

# GETTING FAMILIAR WITH BIG DATA

---

"Data is the new science. Big data holds the answers."

— PAT GELSINGER

---

If you're going into the world of data science, you're going to need to know a little more about big data. As stated earlier, big data is not your average data. The name implies it and it is quite true; big data is larger than the scope of regular data and so entirely deserves its own field of study. This chapter is about helping you understand what big data is, what makes it different, and why it requires big data analytics.

## What Exactly is Big Data?

Big data describes large amounts of raw data obtained from multiple sources. This data aims to make a bold statement and not creep in. Rather, it comes in with a bang at a high velocity and so, it requires a lot of computing power to collect and process.

This type of data is collected through computers, the internet, mobile devices, social media and other electronic and digital means. You and I contribute to the creation of this big data every time we use our smartphones or our computers. These are only a few instances that we contribute to this collection daily. Watching your favorite series on Netflix, ordering food to be delivered to your home and taking an Uber also count as data items collected toward big data collection. All of this data is aimed at one specific purpose - to help businesses with strategic business planning and decision-making.

Before we get down to the nitty-gritty of what big data is, let's take a brief moment to outline the history of big data. Big data has not been around all that long. In fact, it is only about 70 years ago that big data made an emergence into this big, beautiful world of ours with the launch of the first data centers and with relational databases. Still, it had a slow start to being acknowledged. Around 2005, people saw how much unstructured data was generated through social websites like YouTube and Facebook, and other online services did acknowledgment of big data begin. This also led to the development of NoSQL to store data that was not searchable.

Big data continues to make strides because it allows businesses and organizations to gain complete answers that are not available just through processing structured data alone. These answers allow for more well-rounded decision-making as well as the provision of more perspectives on solving difficult problems.

## The Five V's of Big Data

Let's break down what big data means with the five characteristics that differentiate it from your average data. These characteristics all begin with the letter V and so, they are called the three Vs of big data.

## Volume

Volume is defined as the amount of space something occupies. If something has a small volume, it occupies a small amount of space, and the reverse is true for something that has a large volume. The sheer amount of data matters in defining big data as what it is. Big data is most often stored in data lakes. A data lake is a large storage location that houses vast amounts of raw, unprocessed data. Once this data has been processed, it is then moved to a data warehouse, which is a location where data that has already been processed is stored. Big data moves from both of these locations, whose sole existence is to store large amounts of data.

But what is defined as a volume of data large enough to be described as 'big'? Once data becomes too large or too complex for your ordinary computer to process, it has moved into big data. Therefore, big data is a term relative to what current technology can compute on an ordinary basis. In 1999, just 1 gigabyte of data would have been considered big data. That is not even the size of a good-quality movie these days. However, we have computers that far exceed this processing power in our homes in this time and age. Therefore big data only becomes so if it larger than a person or business can store easily, which is around 100 terabytes. Most organizations process hundreds, if not thousands of TB of data.

## Velocity

The next quality that differentiates big data as such is the velocity at which it is received. Velocity describes how quickly something is moving in a given direction. Big data needs to be received quickly and likely be processed just as quickly to fall into that category of data. Therefore, waiting just a few minutes for data to be received from one end to the other might demote this from big data. On the other hand, a computing speed of a few seconds would categorize big data. An example of this ideal speed is when you post a message on Facebook. Almost as soon as you post that message, billions of other people can find it on their feed.

The velocity of the big data is largely dependent on the speed of the internet, which allows for real-time or near real-time receiving of data from one end to the other. This is why there are high-speed internet connections available.

**Variety**

Variety is the quality of being diverse or being different. It takes away the monotony of sameness. Big data encompasses that by having data collected from a variety of different sources and having many types of data encompass its data sets. Traditionally, data was structured neatly and organized in tabular databases. But we live in a time where unstructured and semi-structured data gives as much insight as structured data with proper processing.

Unstructured and semi-structured data types are also encompassed in big data sets along with structured data. This means that big data needs additional processing power to derive meaning from unstructured and semi-structured data types such as audio, video, and text.

Remember that big data has only been around for the last few decades, and it is still evolving as an entity. Therefore, we are still learning about its usefulness. As this education continues, big data has been further differentiating itself from other types of data over the last few years with the addition of two more V's, and they are:

**Bonus-Veracity**

Veracity describes how true something conforms to the facts. In other words, it is about how accurate or how truthful the data is. The value gained from data is only as true as strongly as you can rely on it. Data that has high veracity can be analyzed in a meaningful way that contributes to overall more valuable results in decision-making and planning.

The accuracy of data can get lost in the high volume, high variety and high velocity that is the characteristic of big data. Therefore, it is necessary that the truthfulness of this data be maintained. Structures are being put in place to ensure this, and therefore, this is another characteristic that differentiates big data from traditional data.

## Big Data Analytics vs. Data Analytics

Data analytics is applied to big data just as it is applied to any other type of data. This data needs to be processed and analyzed. Otherwise, how else would it provide valuable insight to companies and organizations? How else would the decision-makers reach conclusions from this raw data? But since it stands to reason that if big data is not like average data, the big data analytics process will be different. So, how does big data analytics differ from your typical data analytics? Let's look at those differences now.

### 1. Nature

Big data analytics is the elevated version of data Analytics. Because of the sheer amount of data being received –processing, analyzing, and interpreting this data needs to be enhanced so that solutions are easier to find. Whereas analytics of traditional data allows the uncovering of answers in a more seamless process, big data analytics needs to dig deeper with more complex processes to uncover the information that is being sought, especially since that message can be lost when new data is constantly coming in at a high speed.

### 2. Structure of data

Traditionally most data is structured. This type of data is structured to fit a format that was determined before it was collected. It is also easily manipulated. This is why the use of SQL databases, with rows and columns, is used to support the storage of this data. The easily manipulatable nature of structured data and the structure in which it is stored make it easy and straightforward to analyze.

Big data consists of structured, unstructured and semi-structured data that are not as easy to manipulate or as easy to store. The analysis of such data is not as straightforward as they cannot be arranged into tables where they would be easily searchable. Traditional data analytics tools are not equipped to handle unstructured and semi-structured data format and complexity. As a result, more complex data analytics tools are necessary. Such tools can include artificial intelligence-powered machines.

### 3. Tools being used

Predictive models and statistical models are the tools used in data analytics with traditional, structured data. These tools are ideal to use in this instance because the relational, tabular nature of structured data makes the data items easy to search out and move between rows and columns.

More complex technology is needed to work with big data. Examples of such tools include parallel computing tools and automation tools. Parallel computing tool refers to machine-powered processes that allow for several calculations or analyses to be done simultaneously. This allows for the acceleration of certain tasks, which is necessary with big data as new data is constantly being added to the data set. Automation tools are software that allows data analytics processes to run with as human interference as possible. The software generates insights and data scientists work with those conclusions.

### 4. Types of industries using big data analytics

There are certain industries where generating terabytes and terabytes of data is commonplace. That is not true for all industries, though. Industries, where it is common for big data to be generated, include healthcare, banking, retail, and IT. Therefore, such industries help pioneer the way forward in the way big data analytics are used.

Other industries that generate fewer bytes of data are less associ-ated with these big data advancements.

## Benefits of Big Data

Any business or organization that generates big data has many activities going on daily. That is the only way such large amounts of data will be generated and received quickly and in so many formats. The data analytics associated with these instances of big data need to keep up with the volume, velocity, and variety of the data being collected.

Once this data analytics process has been fine-tuned, the organiza-tion or business will benefit. Such benefits include:

## Cost Savings

Analyzing big data allows for noting unnecessary costs and thus, implementing strategies that will minimize these costs. This allows the business to operate more efficiently and cost-effectively. Big data also allows for a better understanding of a company's customer base to provide better services, which equates to more profit.

## Product Development

Product development is often done after years of study of the target market. This patience is required because releasing a product the target market does not want is a recipe for loss and disappointment. Analyzing big data allows companies to drill down on what customers truly want, s, they are more likely to develop a winning product.

## Market Insights

All too often, companies are making blind assumptions about what their target consumer base wants out of products. These blind assumptions often lead to missed sales and opportunities. However, companies do not have to lowball themselves in this manner. They can use big data about consumer behavior and marketing trends to stay ahead of the curve and note opportunities that their competition has not noticed yet. The success of Fenty Beauty is a prime example of this, as the executive noticed a shortfall in the beauty industry and provided a more diverse product to fill this gap. They use models from many ethnicities and have a wide range of typically hard-to-match skin tones, developing new formulas that work for all skin types and pinpointing universal shades. Making them known as the "new generation of beauty."

## JOB RESPONSIBILITIES OF BIG DATA PROFESSIONALS

One of the best solutions for solving many of the problems listed above is hiring a big data professional. The job description of big data experts is similar to that of data analysts. The similarity exists because both of these professionals analyze large volumes of data to give insights to businesses and organizations so that concise conclusions are met. Big data professional job descriptions are often more weighted with additional responsibilities such as collecting, interpreting, analyzing and reporting on a larger scale in addition to helping companies and organizations maintain software and hardware that allow for higher levels of accessibility, usability and security of big data. Data scientists are usually at the forefront of working with big data.

To break it down further, the responsibilities of big data professionals include:

- The analysis of real-time situations. Big data always comes in quickly and constantly and leaving this data sitting neutral will be of no value to businesses and organizations. This data needs to be processed as soon as possible, oftentimes as immediately as they are collected. Big data professionals are the ones who help businesses and organizations stay on the ball by making use of this data as they facilitate the analysis and interpretation of real-time situations so that conclusions are met without delay.

- The development of systems that allow the processing of data on a large scale. Remember that big data is composed of structured, unstructured, and semi-structured data. This collection of a multitude of types of data needs to be stored and processed so that all of it is easy to retrieve and interpret. This storage and processing need to be comprised of both software and hardware components that are best suited for the particular needs of businesses and organizations. Big data professionals help develop well-rounded systems that better analyze all types of big data received so that better decisions are made.

- The detection of fraudulent transactions and outliers. We live in a time where fraudulent activity is commonplace and ever-increasing. These fraudulent activities are often detected in big data collection, but that is only possible if this big data is monitored data. Big data professionals help data owners, especially in industries such as the banking and security sectors that handle sensitive content, detect fraudulent activities and transactions. The monitoring of big data also allows for the detection of outliers that can mean a change in the direction of decision-making for businesses and organizations.

## Top 10 Big Data Tools You Should Know About

Big data cannot be adequately stored or processed through your traditional data analytic means. Special tools are needed for all the processes that allow for the ultimate use of this big data.

Whether you are a big data owner or a big data professional, you need to become familiar with a few common tools to store, process, and analyze big data with as much efficiency and accuracy as possible. Don't worry. You don't have to learn them all at once. Different companies use different tools, so you'll slowly gain familiarity throughout your career. Some of these tools include:

- **Apache Hadoop**, which is open-source software that boasts several functions that allow the storage, processing, and resource management of data. It is written in the programming language Java and is one of the most popular big data processing tools. There is a major drawback to this tool, it does not allow real-time data processing.
- **Apache Spark**, which is a tool that is equally as popular as Hadoop. This is because it overcomes the drawbacks of the previous software with real-time processing. It also allows batch processing of data just like Hadoop does.
- **Apache Storm**, which is also an open-source big data tool. It's popularity is attributable to the fact that it allows for the processing of unbounded streams of data, which refers to data that is constantly coming in with no definitive end.
- **Apache Cassandra**, which is a database that is perfect for processing all data types. With this tool, you do not have to worry about storing structured, unstructured, and semi-structured data types in different locations.
- **MongoDB**, which is a NoSQL database data analytics tool that is user-friendly and cost-effective. It is written the programming languages JavaScript, C, and C++ and is great for use in big data infrastructures that are cloud-based.
- **Apache Flink**, which is a data analytics tool that is used for both bounded (data that comes in with a

definitive end) and unbounded data streams. It is also open-source and quick to recover from faults that occur in the data architecture.

- **Apache Kafka**, which is a streaming platform that allows for the output of big data with guaranteed zero downtime. LinkedIn launched this open-source platform in 2011.

- **Tableau,** which is a data visualization tool that quickly turns raw data into valuable insights. It is user-friendly and does not require any programming or technical skills to use.

- **Rapidminer**, which is a tool that facilitates machine learning, data analytic processes, and data science processes in one powerful tool. This is an open-source tool that can be integrated with cloud services and APIs

- **R programming**, written in the open-source programming language R, this tool allows for the computation of complex statistical operations to enhance data analysis.

# Expanding Your Knowledge From Home? Check Out Some World-Class Courses and Job-Ready Certificate Programs From Coursera!

Scan the QR codes with your mobile device or visit the links to see whats right for you.

Your path to a career in data science **—no experience necessary.**

# Checkout Some Courses

## General Data Analysis Courses
Link:imp.i384100.net/DataAnalysis

## SQL Courses
Link:imp.i384100.net/SQLCourse

## Excel For Data Analysis Courses
Link:imp.i384100.net/ExcelData

## Machine Learning Courses
Link: imp.i384100.net/MachineLearningData

## Python For Data Analysis Courses
Link: imp.i384100.net/PythonForData

## Data Visualization with Tableau
Link:imp.i384100.net/Tableau

## Full Data Science Certificates
Link:imp.i384100.net/DataScienceSpecialization

## 12
# CAREER GUIDANCE

---

"Data will talk to you, if you're willing to listen"

— JIM BERGESON

---

The world of data holds a wealth of opportunities for anyone brave enough to delve in and make learning a priority. From the tree of data science, there are several paths that you can take to develop a career. If you're still in the process of finding a career and want to dive deeper, this chapter discusses some of the leading career paths and allows you to analyze which one of these might be right for you. It's possible to land a career as a data analyst with knowledge in SQL, Python, Excel, etc. However, many higher-level jobs such as data scientists require some level of higher education such as a bachelor's in math, statistics, computer science, economics, engineering, or anything similar. Due your due diligence and find out what is required for your desired field. If you're already working in data and are happy with your path, feel free to skip to the conclusion.

## DATA ANALYST

Average Salary: $63,456 (Source: Payscale.com as of 2022)

There is no doubt about it. Becoming a data analyst is one of the most common directions that any person interested in the field of data first thinks of. If you:

- Like working with numbers
- Understand the mechanics of coding with languages such as Python or R
- Understand the significance of communication skills in this field just as importantly as you understand the vital contribution of mathematics toward data

...then becoming a data analyst might just be the career path for you.

But what exactly is it that data analysts do? Let's break it down. There is actually quite a lot involved in this career and some of the tasks include:

- Gather data
- Clean data
- Model data
- Present data

To simplify things, data analysts transform data into clear, concise insights that are used to make decisions and plan strategies. This means the presentation of data visuals is a vital part of this career. Because of this, data analysts need to develop expert-level skills when it comes to the manipulation of data fit for communication to others by using all of the tools available to them. Excel is one of the most commonly used tools, so understanding and deriving information from spreadsheets quickly and efficiently is a must.

The use of Microsoft Excel is one of the first steps that many startup companies take to start the development of databases. Excel is typically adequate as they have not accumulated as much data as bigger companies and organizations. Excel is equipped with enough features that allow for storage of moderately-sized databases in addition to quick data analytics. Learning to use Excel is typically one of the first steps that data analysts take. Once they have mastered this, they move on to more advanced database start-ups like SQL, Python, and R programming.

Other must-have skills of data analysts include:

## Programming Languages

SQL: Many companies and organizations use SQL databases to store, access, and manage data. For example, payroll is handled in such a database. Retail companies store information about products in such databases as well.

Python or R (even both): Both of these programming languages can perform advanced data analytics on large sets of data. Knowledge of either of these programs is well respected in the world of data.

As stated earlier, Python is more user-friendly and easier to learn but learning either or both of these two programs is suitable when pursuing a career as a data analyst.

## Critical Thinking

Data is of no use to anyone if the data analyst cannot view this with a critical eye and ask the right questions to find possible answers to the problems a business or organization might face. Therefore, to be successful as a data analyst, you need to develop your critical thinking skills.

## Data Visualization

Remember that a huge part of a data analyst's job is to make data presentations to other people to aid in decision-making. As a result, this person needs to be able to develop a great narrative and tell a compelling data story that mobilizes the audience to act on the solutions provided with a problem. My recommendation for this is Tableau's visualization software. This tool allows the creation of attention-grabbing charts and graphs to enhance your data story.

## Presentation Skills

Your data visualizations will fall flat if you do not have the presentation skills to enhance them. Don't be alarmed if presenting to groups of people doesn't come naturally to you. It does not to most people. Luckily, this is something that you can work on and improve so that you can become more comfortable as time passes by. There are plenty of courses and classes to help with this but nothing beats experience. The more you do it, the better you will become at it.

DATA SCIENTIST

Average Salary: $97,665 (Source: Payscale.com as of 2022)

Being a data scientist involves a mathematical, statistical and programming background to develop the skills necessary for analyzing data and creating mathematical models that can be applied to data collection, storage and processing. Becoming a data scientist involves using analytic skills to develop trends and manage data collection and processing. Data scientists typically develop these skills in a niche-specific way to specialize within that industry. For example, some data scientists develop skills that are particular to the healthcare industry, while others develop skills best suited for the IT industry. No matter what industry a data scientist specializes in, their role within an organization or business is to develop a contextual understanding of the data accumulated in that industry and that specific company for more effective decision-making and the development of strategic plans.

With typical majors such as mathematics, computer science, physics, and economics, even if a data scientist develops niche-specific skills, all data scientists start off learning the same skills. The skillset required of data scientists is more than those required of a data analyst. Must have skills of data scientists include:

- Fluent in Python and R programming languages
- SQL Databases
- Big Data storage and processing programs
- Machine learning
- Data visualization and software need to make winning presentations
- Business strategy
- Math and statistics
- Data modeling

We have already discussed most of these and their application to a data career above. Let us touch on those we have not discussed yet; business strategy, big data programs for storage and processing, and data modeling.

## Business Strategy

To help companies and organizations create the most effective business strategies, a data scientist must understand business-specific problems, conduct analysis of those problems, and spearhead the way to engineering solutions to solve these problems. Encompassed within the development of business strategy skills, acquiring other skills is necessary and that list includes analytic skills, problem-solving skills, communication skills, and planning and management skills. Data scientists need to get a handle on all of these as they are the foundation for thinking with a strategic business mindset. Luckily, all of these skills can be developed with time by asking strategic questions, learning to take a step back and observing data, learning to leverage opposing ideas to reach the common, beneficial ground and of course, embracing the development of formal skills.

## Big Data Programs for Storage and Processing

With so much big data being generated every single day, collecting and processing big data is something every data scientist will encounter if he or she hopes to grow within this field. As a result, learning to make use of the tools that streamline collecting and processing big data is a must. We have discussed many of these in the previous chapter, such as Hadoop and Spark. My suggestion is to pursue becoming familiar with each of the programs listed in the previous chapter. Do not overwhelm yourself. Take pursuing this education one platform or software at a time if possible.

## Data Modeling

Data modeling describes the process of finding and analyzing the parameters necessary to support the collection and processing of data that supports the overall achievement of a business or organization's goals. This process needs to define how data sets relate to each other and how the resulting insights are generated. Without the provision of these parameters, chaos will ensue and obtaining concise, helpful insights from that data will become impossible. Data scientists are tasked with developing these parameters and locating the tools that will ensure that these parameters are kept no matter how much data is collected or how quickly that is done.

Because data scientists tend to need a broader set of skills but to encompass aiding businesses and organizations with the theory, implementation, and communication of data systems, they tend to be compensated higher than data analysts.

## DATA ENGINEER

Average Salary: $93,623 (Source: Payscale.com as of 2022)

Data engineers specialize in creating software solutions that surround the collection and processing of big data. This means that data engineers are responsible for paving a way to ensure that big data is usable and accessible to the right persons. They are the ones responsible for ensuring that data is secure and adds value to companies and organizations. They are the ones who are able to transform all types of big data into usable insights. Whereas data scientists focus on extracting value from data, data engineers are the ones who develop the infrastructure that allows the extraction of this value. Data engineers focus on the architecture of data generation as well. This is a contrast to data scientists whose tasks focus more on advanced mathematics and statistical processes that transform the data generated by the infrastructure and architecture data engineers develop. Even though data scientists are constantly engaged with interacting with this data infrastructure and architecture, data engineers claim praise for building and maintaining systems.

Still, the skillsets needed in these careers tend to overlap. Must-have skills that they share include:

- Knowledge of both SQL and NoSQL database systems
- Knowledge of programming languages such as Python and R.
- Understanding the basics of distributed systems
- Understanding the basics of machine learning and the related algorithms and data structures

Soft skills such as collaboration skills, presentation skills, and communication skills

It should be noted that data engineers tend to rely on additional programming languages such as Java and Scala. Java Is an object-oriented, general-purpose programming language that is designed to have a smooth implementation. Scala works in a similar way. Therefore, learning both or either of these programming languages will benefit data engineers greatly.

Additional skills that data engineers need include:

## Understanding and Implementing Data Warehousing Solutions

A data warehouse is a database where big data has accumulated from a wide range of sources. Such as system relies on efficient reporting and data analysis so that this big data is ultimately used to generate meaningful insights. Data engineers need to be able to implement both the software and hardware components that go into efficiently creating such a system.

## Implementing ETL Tools

ETL stands for extract, transform and load. This is the process that is used to copy data from one location or source into another while ensuring that the integrity of this data is maintained. This is a vital database function used for data cleaning and the combination of data from several sources. Data engineers set up the parameters of this function to ensure that this integrity is maintained.

## Understanding and Implementing Data APIs

As a reminder, API stands for application programming interface. This is the software architecture that allows accessing data and the applications that go into its management. APIs are the protocols that allow data to be transmitted between different software products without compromising the data's integrity. Data engineers aid in setting up these data APIs.

## DATA ARCHITECT

Average Salary: $123,754 (Source: Payscale.com as of 2022)

Data architects are the ones who envision and design the framework to manage a business or organization's data needs and conceptualize how these needs will be fulfilled. This means this person helps with the planning, specification of parameters, enabling, maintenance, access, cleaning, control, and more of the data systems. Think of data architects as the ones who translate the wants of businesses into the data specifications that it will take to fulfill these needs. Envision it just like with the design of a house. Structural architects take the requirements of the house owners that need to be built, such as the layout and the number of bedrooms, and translate those needs into plans that the engineers can understand and thus, turn into reality.

This means that data architects work closely with data engineers. While the data architect is responsible for creating the blueprint for the data systems, the data engineers are the one who builds it.

Because the world of data is still evolving, the role of the data architect is also still changing. Many data architects are still learning on the job. But there are still some basic skills that data architects must have. They include:

- Knowledge and development of SQL and NoSQL databases.
- Knowledge and development of systems development life cycles. A system development life cycle looks like this:
- Planning
- System analysis
- System design
- System development
- Implementation

- Integration
- Testing
- Operations
- Maintenance
- A data architect needs to oversee and implement all of these parts of a data systems development life cycle.
- Proficiency of data modeling and design of the systems that encompass that.
- Proficiency in predictive modeling. This means developing predictions about future events based on trends and insights gained from data collected. Data architects develop systems to make this as efficient as possible for enhanced decision-making.
- Knowledge of programming languages such as Python and Java. Acquiring knowledge of additional programming languages such as C, C++, and Perl is also a plus. Perl is feature-rich and has been around for over 30 years. C and C++ are general-purpose languages that support advanced statistical operation as well the input of structured data.
- Knowledge of NLP (natural language programming.) This programming language is a subfield of computer science, linguistics and artificial intelligence. This subfield focuses on studying the interaction between human languages and machines. As it relates to data, the focus is on how computers process data input in the form of natural human language. The development of this field is to make it so that computers can efficiently analyze the unstructured data input of human speech.
- Proficiency in text analysis. This involves developing and maintaining processes and systems that can obtain relevant data from text data like emails and tweets. This is a machine learning technique.
- Project management approaches and requirements. The task of designing the blueprint for an entire data system

is no small feat. The normal person will get lost in the nuances that go into this and quit. However, data architects need to be able to design a plan for moving from one step to the next effortlessly. That is where being efficient at project management comes in clutch.

## MORE CAREERS

The career titles listed above are only a few more sought-after jobs available in the world of data. There are so many more that you can branch off into. It is best to explore and find the one that appeals to you and tailor your education and experience towards achieving that discipline. Some of the other job titles within the data career include:

### Business Intelligence Analyst

Average Salary: $71,493 (Source: Payscale.com as of 2022)

BI Analysts focus on utilizing data and information to improve an organization. After they gather, organize and analyze internal and external company data, they use that information to identify trends, issues, and patterns to turn their analysis into actionable strategies the business can implement.

### Senior Business Analyst

Average Salary: $87,131 (Source: Payscale.com as of 2022)

One of the most pursued sub-careers in data analytics is business analytics. Business analysts focus their efforts more on the business applications in data and actions that can enhance the efficiency and productivity of businesses and organizations. Their efforts give insight into how companies should make investments, approach marketing, and product development, to name a few. Essentially, Business analysts use data and current business metrics to make strategic business decisions. Data analysts gather data, manipulate it, identify useful information, and transform their findings into digestible insights.

## Marketing Analyst

Average Salary:$58,375 (Source: Payscale.com as of 2022)

Marketing Analysts help their company better understand their market. They tend to analyze data sets, do market research, customer surveys, and monitor purchasing trends to identify their target market. They then can develop strategies to help companies better meet and connect with new and existing customers. They then present these findings to leadership and managers through reports and visualizations.

## Machine Learning Engineer

Average Salary: $112,792 (Source: Payscale.com as of 2022)

This career is related to creating and implementing software solutions to solve problems related to data storage and processing.

# Thank you so much for making it this far!

I greatly appreciate the time you took to give my book a read. As a small indie publisher, it means a lot and I hope I am making a difference in your career.

If you have 60 seconds, it would mean the world to me if you could leave a short review on Amazon. It does wonders for the book and i love hearing how you benefited from it!

## To leave your feedback:

1. Open your camera app
2. Point your mobile device at the QR code below
3. The review page will appear in your web browser

Or

Visit Review2.elizabethsclarke.com

*Thank you!*

# CONCLUSION

There are instances where just one byte of data is more valuable than a brick of gold. Imagine the value that can be derived from zettabytes of data being generated every year. Technology is growing fast and with it, the bytes of data are streaming in faster and faster and in formats and volume that could not have been interpreted just a few decades ago.

Businesses and individuals worldwide have recognized that data is not what it used to be - confined to rows and columns in tabular form. Instead, voice notes, tweets, text, videos and so many more data forms also contribute to the makeup of all these zettabytes of data. These forms of data are outside of the convention and they are a large reason why the value of data is climbing every single day.

However, all of this data is useless until it is transformed from its raw state into insights that lead to reasonable decision-making and plans that translate into the billions of dollars that this industry is now worth. This value is still growing every single year. Remember that the data industry is expected to exceed $77 billion by the end of 2023. Imagine the global value of this industry as big data and data analytics are just part of the data world. Now imagine the value that cannot be measured. The value that comes from the piece of making decisions is based on sound research and information. Imagine the security of knowing that these decisions are based on facts and trends instead of mere hunches and assumptions.

As a data analyst, data engineer, data architect, or carrying any of the other career titles in this industry, imagine how you can be part of developing that value. You can be a part of the revolution that allows for the use of all of this data, since more than 80% of it remains unused and therefore, without developed value. In this day and age of the ever-increasing advancements made in technologies like artificial intelligence, machine learning and more, there is no limit to the possibilities of what we can achieve by using data and thus, developing each byte to its fullest potential.

You can help move this industry towards growth and prosperity and be part of one of the most important decades for data.

# More Books From the Author

**Scan with phone camera**

**Scan with phone camera**

Join My Mailing List at
ElizabethSClarke.com to Stay Up to Date
for Future Releases and Promos!

# 13

# BONUS CHAPTER -
# INTRODUCTION TO STATISTICS
# AND PROBABILITY

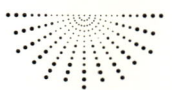

---

"I keep saying that the sexy job in the next 10 years will be statisticians, and I'm not kidding"

— HAL VARIAN

---

For any of you dedicated folks wanting a quick introduction to statistics read on!

Part of the numerical literacy that every data scientist must have is knowledge of statistics and probability. Not only that, but every data scientist must know how to apply those numerical functions. The first step to getting to that height is to understand what each of these terms means and how they are applied in the world of data. So, jump right into those explanations.

First up, let's take a look at statistics. Statistics revolves around collecting, analyzing, interpreting and presenting data. The entire point of using statistics is to show how the data that has been collected, analyzed, interpreted and presented can be used to solve a particular problem. We have plenty of statistics on world poverty. Why? To ultimately solve the problem of world poverty. Companies have statistics on customer retention and how well marketing campaigns are working. Why? To improve sales.

Population and sample are two of the most frequently used terms in statistics. Population refers to a data set whose features and variables need to be analyzed. Samples are subgroups within the population. Samples are used to gain the most accurate information to highlight the qualities of the population as a whole. Therefore, samples need to be chosen effectively.

Luckily, to achieve this sample as best as possible, you are not left up to your own devices, nor do you have to play a game of eeny, meeny, minee, moe. Instead, you can use the techniques known as probability sampling or non-probability sampling.

When using probability sampling, samples are chosen using the theory of probability. That leads to an explanation on what probability is. Probability describes the characteristic of how likely something is to happen. Therefore, these techniques of sampling rely on that characteristic. There are three main types of probability sampling are:

- **Random sampling**, which is based on the theory that any data item of the population has an equal chance of being selected to represent this population in that sample. Data items are selected at random to make this representation.
- **Systematic sampling**, which is based on data items being chosen based on a certain characteristic to be part of the sample. For example, data items may be chosen based on whether they are an odd number or an even number to be part of the sample.
- **Stratified sampling**, which is based on picking data items to be part of the sample based on a stratum. A stratum is a subgroup within a population that shares at

least one feature in common. Once that subgroup is determined, then random sampling is used to determine the final number of data items that will be part of the sample.

Non-probability sampling does not give data items on the population an equal chance of being selected for analysis. Non-probability sampling is in a whole other ballpark and very complex. Therefore, we will not go into much detail about it in this book.

There are two main types of statistics. They are:

## Descriptive Statistics

This type of statistics describes certain characteristics of a set of data and thus, giving short summaries about the sample used to represent the population. Words that you will come across frequently used to make these descriptions include average, minimum, and maximum.

## Inferential Statistics

This type of statistics is used to make predictions about a population based on the sample taken to make their representation. Rather than giving precise descriptions, inferential statistics make generalizations about the population and use probability to back the conclusion made. Therefore, you may hear more vague descriptions such as small, medium and large, used in creating conclusions based on inferential statistics.

LET's take a moment to look at the relationship between statistics and probability. The two areas are related as probability shows the prediction of the likelihood of events happening in the future, while statistics allows the production of this probability by analyzing the frequency of past events. Probability is the engine that drives the vehicle of statistics. Therefore, to solidify your understanding of statistics, it is only right that we delve deeper into what probability is.

I have stated that probability is a measure of how likely something is to happen. Still, in business, probability is more aptly defined as how likely the desired outcome is compared to the total number of outcomes possible. The formula for this looks like this:

**(desired outcomes) / (total outcomes)**

Unfortunately, sometimes outcomes cannot be predicted absolutely and that is known as a random experiment.

Other terms that you will come across in your study of probability include:

- Sample space is the total number of outcomes possible in a random experiment.
- Event, which describes one or more outcomes that are possible with an experiment.
- Disjoint event, which is a type of event described as not connected. That is, events that cannot happen at the same time. An example of this would be to toss a coin and get heads and tails simultaneously, which is an impossibility.
- Non-disjoint event, which is a type of event that has common outcomes. An example of this would be a basket player throwing the ball 25 times to make a basket every time.
- Probability distribution, which describes all the possible outcomes that may occur with a random event within a given set of parameters.

There are three main probability distribution functions: probability density function, normal distribution and central limit theorem.

## Probability Density Function

This describes the likelihood of a continuous random variable occurring within particular parameters of the sample. Continuous random variables speak to the quality of having an infinite number of possible values. Because of this, the probability density function is often used to gauge the risk/reward probability of investments such as stock and ETFs.

## Normal Distribution

This describes the continuous probability distribution around a central peak. This peak shows the mean or average distribution of variables within that sample. Averages on either end of this distribution are less dense, showing a lesser likelihood to occur. When depicted on a graph, this type of probability is bell-shaped to show a higher concentration around the mean. An example of normal distribution can be the average height of 30 boys within a particular grade in elementary school. More than likely, the heights of these boys will be centralized around a mean peak while there will be a few boys who are shorter or taller than this average. This also goes by the name Gaussian distribution.

## Central Limit Theorem

This describes the theory that if a large population is divided into several samples, then these samples' average will be equal or almost equal. In other words, the central limit theorem describes the characteristic of normal distribution perpetrating itself regardless of how large this population gets.

THANK you for sticking around this long! Make sure to grab your free checklist by joining my email list at ElizabethSClarke.com and stay up to date with all future releases!

# RESOURCES

Akhtar, Z. (2020, August 17). 5 basic components of data science. Retrieved from https://databasetown.com/basic-components-of-data-science/

Bad data costs the U.S. $3 trillion per year. (2016, September 22). Retrieved from https://hbr.org/2016/09/bad-data-costs-the-u-s-3-trillion-per-year

A complete tutorial on statistics and probability. (2020, April 24). Retrieved from https://www.edureka.co/blog/statistics-and-probability/#What%20Is%20Statistics

Corporate Finance Institute. (2021, July 27). Data analytics. Retrieved from https://corporatefinanceinstitute.com/resources/knowledge/other/data-analytics

Data analytics vs data analysis: What's the difference? (n.d.). Retrieved from https://www.bmc.com/blogs/data-analytics-vs-data-analysis/

Data collection: Purpose, methods, and tools for great decision making. (2019, November 20). Retrieved from https://upskillnation.com/data-collection/

A data literacy guide for D&A leaders. (n.d.). Retrieved from https://www.gartner.com/smarterwithgartner/a-data-and-analytics-leaders-guide-to-data-literacy

Guide to data cleaning: Definition, benefits, components, and how to clean your data. (n.d.). Retrieved from https://www.tableau.com/learn/articles/what-is-data-cleaning

Hao, K. (2018, November 17). What is machine learning? Retrieved from https://www.technologyreview.com/2018/11/17/103781/what-is-machine-learning-we-drew-you-another-flowchart/

Machine learning for data analysis. (2020, August 7). Retrieved from https://www.udacity.com/blog/2020/08/machine-learning-for-data-analysis.html

Machine learning: Applications of artificial intelligence to imaging and diagnosis. (n.d.). Retrieved from https://www.ncbi.nlm.nih.gov/pmc/articles/PMC6381354/

Requirements of data visualisation tools to analyse big data: A structured literature review. (n.d.). Retrieved from https://www.ncbi.nlm.nih.gov/pmc/articles/PMC7134219/

Seven characteristics that define quality data. (2018, November 30). Retrieved from https://blazent.com/seven-characteristics-define-quality-data/

Types of data analysis. (2018, February 23). Retrieved from https://chartio.com/learn/data-analytics/types-of-data-analysis/

What is data management and why is it important? (2019, October 30). Retrieved from https://searchdatamanagement.techtarget.com/definition/data-management

What is data science? (2021, October 25). Retrieved from https://ischoolonline.berkeley.edu/data-science/what-is-data-science/

Why is data visualization important? What is important in data visualization? · Issue 2.1, winter 2020. (2020, January 31). Retrieved from https://hdsr.mitpress.mit.edu/pub/zok97i7p/release/3

Z. (2020, May 19). *4 Examples of Using Linear Regression in Real Life*. Statology. Retrieved March 31, 2022, from https://www.statology.org/linear-regression-real-life-examples/#:%7E:text=Linear%20Regression%20Real%20Life%20Example%20%232,how%20their%20blood%20pressure%20responds.

Singh, J. (2019, October 8). *7 Real-Life Examples of How Business Intelligence Can Transform a Business [Update]*. RTS Labs. Retrieved March 31, 2022, from https://rtslabs.com/7-real-life-examples-of-how-business-intelligence-can-transform-a-business/

deBara, D. (2021, February 2). *Data Professionals Are in High Demand—Here Are 8 Jobs You Should Consider*. The Muse. Retrieved February 31, 2022, from https://www.themuse.com/advice/data-and-analytics-jobs-careers

Digital Vidya. (2021, April 23). *8 Ways To Clean Data Using Data Cleaning Techniques*. Retrieved February 31, 2022, from https://www.digitalvidya.com/blog/data-cleaning-techniques/

Morris, A. (2021, April 16). *23 Case Studies and Real-World Examples of How Business Intelligence Keeps Top Companies Competitive*. Oracle NetSuite. Retrieved March 31, 2022, from https://www.netsuite.com/portal/resource/articles/business-strategy/business-intelligence-examples.shtml

PCMag. (n.d.). *Definition of relational query*. Retrieved February 31, 2022, from https://www.pcmag.com/encyclopedia/term/relational-query

Morrow, M. M. (2020, November 4). *How Businesses Use Transactional Data to Drive Growth*. Hubworks. Retrieved March 31,

2022, from https://altametrics.com/en/sales-forecast/transactional-data.html

Trevino, A. T. (2016, December 26). *Introduction to K-means Clustering*. Oracle AI & Data Science Blog. Retrieved March 31, 2022, from https://blogs.oracle.com/ai-and-datascience/post/introduction-to-k-means-clustering

Z. (2020b, October 26). *Introduction to Simple Linear Regression*. Statology. Retrieved March 31, 2022, from https://www.statology.org/linear-regression/

P. (2021, August 26). *K Means Clustering | K Means Clustering Algorithm in Python*. Analytics Vidhya. Retrieved March 31, 2022, from https://www.analyticsvidhya.com/blog/2019/08/comprehensive-guide-k-means-clustering/

Jeffares, A. (2021, December 12). *K-means: A Complete Introduction - Towards Data Science*. Medium. Retrieved March 31, 2022, from https://towardsdatascience.com/k-means-a-complete-introduction-1702af9cd8c

S. (2020a, December 2). *Linear vs Logistic Regression | Linear and Logistic Regression*. Analytics Vidhya. Retrieved March 31, 2022, from https://www.analyticsvidhya.com/blog/2020/12/beginners-take-how-logistic-regression-is-related-to-linear-regression/

Agrawal, A. (2020, February 14). *Logistic Regression. Simplified. - Data Science Group, IITR*. Medium. Retrieved March 31, 2022, from https://medium.com/data-science-group-iitr/logistic-regression-simplified-9b4efe801389

Yi, M. (2019, October 16). *A Complete Guide to Scatter Plots*. Chartio. Retrieved March 31, 2022, from https://chartio.com/learn/charts/what-is-a-scatter-plot/

Smallcombe, M. (2020, June 17). *Structured vs Unstructured Data: 5 Key Differences*. Integrate.Io. Retrieved March 31, 2022, from https://www.integrate.io/blog/structured-vs-unstructured-data-key-differences/#:%7E:text=The%20term%20structured%20data%20refers,it's%20within%20an%20RDBMS %20structure .

Elgabry, O. (2019, February 28). *The Ultimate Guide to Data Cleaning - Towards Data Science*. Medium. Retrieved March 31, 2022, from https://towardsdatascience.com/the-ultimate-guide-to-data-cleaning-3969843991d4

Dawar, H. (2021, May 25). *Types of Variables in Data Science! - Geek Culture*. Medium. Retrieved March 31, 2022, from https://medium.com/geekculture/types-of-variables-in-data-science-eb34739589b2

E. (2020a, July 24). *Understanding K-means Clustering with Examples*. Edureka. Retrieved March 31, 2022, from https://www.edureka.co/blog/k-means-clustering/

A. (2020a, July 18). *Understanding The Linear Regression!!!! - Analytics Vidhya*. Medium. Retrieved March 31, 2022, from https://medium.com/analytics-vidhya/understanding-the-linear-regression-808c1f69441c0

Kovačević, A. (2021, June 10). *What Is a Relational Database?* Knowledge Base by phoenixNAP. Retrieved March 31, 2022, from https://phoenixnap.com/kb/what-is-a-relational-database

Fruhlinger, P. M. J. K. (2019, October 16). *What is business intelligence? Transforming data into business insights*. CIO. Retrieved March 31, 2022, from https://www.cio.com/article/272364/business-intelligence-definition-and-solutions.html

Gramlich, M. (2022, September 9). *What is structured, semi structured and unstructured data? › Michael Gramlich*. Michael Gramlich. Retrieved March 31, 2022, from https://www.michael-gramlich.com/what-is-structured-semi-structured-and-unstructured-data/

Piech, C. P. (n.d.). *CS221*. Stanford Cs221. Retrieved March 31, 2022, from https://stanford.edu/%7Ecpiech/cs221/handouts/kmeans.html

Saini, A. (2021, August 31). *Decision Tree Algorithm - A Complete Guide*. Analytics Vidhya. Retrieved March 31, 2022, from https://www.analyticsvidhya.com/blog/2021/08/decision-tree-algorithm/

Meyerson, M. (2021, August 27). *Regression analysis to improve Google Ads performance*. Search Engine Land. Retrieved March 31, 2022, from https://searchengineland.com/regression-analysis-to-improve-google-ads-performance-313898

Sánchez, P. (2018, February 7). *Data cleansing & data transformation*. Quantdare. Retrieved March 31, 2022, from https://quantdare.com/data-cleansing-and-transformation/

GraphPad Software, LLC. (n.d.). *GraphPad Prism 9 Curve Fitting Guide - Example: Simple logistic regression*. GraphPad. Retrieved March 31, 2022, from https://www.graphpad.com/guides/prism/latest/curve-fitting/reg_simple_logistic_example.htm

Made in United States
North Haven, CT
23 January 2023

31523074R00090